TONY MACAULAY grew up in Belfast during the Troubles – an experience that has shaped his life and inspired his writing. He has spent more than thirty years working for peace in Northern Ireland and abroad. Today he works as a leadership consultant to global organisations and is a regular contributor to BBC Radio. He is the author of three bestselling *Breadboy* and *All Growed Up*.

PRAISE FOR TONY MACAULAY

'Macaulay has succeeded in shining a powerful light into the lives of ordinary people and how they coped with circumstances of extraordinary brutality ... a tale full of courage and optimism, and simple niceness.'

Maurice Hayes, *Irish Independent*

'Tony Macaulay gets behind the stereotypes and shows life as it was ...'

Belfast Telegraph

TONY MACAULAY

LITTLE HOUSE ON THE PEACE LINE

LIVING AND WORKING AS A PACIFIST ON BELFAST'S MURDER MILE

·THE·
BLACK
·STAFF·
PRESS

First published in 2017 by Blackstaff Press
an imprint of Colourpoint Creative Ltd
Colourpoint House
Jubilee Business Park
21 Jubilee Road
Newtownards BT23 4YH

With the assistance of
The Arts Council of Northern Ireland

Tony Macaulay has asserted his right under the
Copyright, Designs and Patents Act 1988 to be
identified as the author of this work.

Typeset by KT Designs, St Helens, England

Printed in Berwick-upon-Tweed by Martins the Printers

A CIP catalogue for this book is available from the British Library

ISBN 978 0 85640 992 9

www.blackstaffpress.com

Follow Tony on Twitter @tonymacaulay

Some names and identifying details have been changed
to protect the privacy of individuals.

For Billy

CONTENTS

PROLOGUE

GO TELL IT ON THE MOUNTAIN!

'Watch yourself, son. It changes dead quick round here, so it does,' shouts the rugged dog walker. I can just about hear him over the gusting wind.

Change and quick are not words I associate with my beloved city. I've spent most of my life having to watch myself for wanting this place to change too fast.

In 1998, nationalist and unionist politicians agreed to share power in Northern Ireland but today their voters still aren't sure if they want to live together. My hopes for past hurts healed and a city at ease with its different peoples are still not a reality. My dreams of Catholics and Protestants and people of all faiths living together in shared streets and our children learning together in the same schools have not come true. But then I always was a bit of dreamer.

'That wee lad's head's in cloud cuckoo land,' my mother would say, fretting as she watched me grow up hoping for peace with our Catholic neighbours across the peace wall in West Belfast. She knew very well that things did not change very quickly.

'Thanks. I'm going for a hike up to the Black Mountain ridge,'

I reply to the walker as if I were Sir Edmund Hillary – but in truth I have little of the requisite skill, muscle or mountaineering equipment. For my ascent of Divis Mountain I'm wearing an old pair of jeans, prehistoric trainers, a faded Doctor Who fiftieth anniversary T-shirt and an inappropriately youthful hoodie, which at least prevents the wind from puncturing my eardrums.

'Ah sure, you'll be all right, mate,' calls the dog walker. 'Them there clouds over the Mournes is goin' nowhere, so they're nat.'

I assume he's a fellow West Belfast man about the same age as me, but as the entrance to the Divis Mountain park is closer to the nationalist area, he's probably from the other side of the sectarian divide. As if that matters. In fifty years time we'll both be on the other 'other side'. In a thousand years, if archeologists dig up our bones, they won't identify us as Irish or British, just human remains. My compatriot looks like he's had a tougher life than me and, as he tugs on his pit bull terrier's leash, I wonder what experiences have carved those deep grooves in his tanned forehead. In any case I accept his superior meteorological knowledge, as I haven't been up here in thirty years. It's early summer and, apart from a few clouds threatening in the distance, the sky is lighter and bluer than I could have imagined. Due to a lifelong problem of trying to cram too much into my diary, I have exactly ninety minutes to reach the summit or I'll be late for a recording of a television interview with another Belfast writer.

At nearly sixteen hundred feet, Divis Mountain (from the Irish *Dubhais*, meaning 'black back') is the highest and darkest of our hills over Belfast. It's a wild and barren place, breathing down the neck of the vast housing estates of West Belfast. I'm certain most of the residents have never been up here – even though it's their mountain and the need to claim ownership of land is visceral for the people of Belfast. Seventy years ago thousands of families, including my father's, climbed up these fields to escape the Belfast Blitz. Of course, I cannot help but recall the dirty war that broke out in the streets below in 1969 when I was only six years old.

I grew up at the top of the Shankill Road in one of the new 1960s housing estates that crept up the mountain. Our red-brick homes encroached on the green fields lush with gorse and heather that slope upwards steeply to mountaintop moorland. When I was a child we called this adventure zone 'up the fields'. All summer long we climbed over bushes, marshy sheughs and fields covered in cows' clap, picking blackberries and catching newts in streams en route to the summit. It was a hard climb for a wee lad to reach the mountaintop past angry farmers, irritable bulls and suspicious soldiers. Even back then, you had to watch yourself round here.

It's a good indication of how Belfast has risen from the ashes of thirty-five years of conflict that this mountain, once controlled by the British Army as a strategic vantage point overlooking hostile territory, now belongs to the National Trust and has a proper car park, picnic tables and a visitors' centre. The last time I was up here there were 'Keep Out' signs and helicopters and soldiers. Today there are signs for scenic nature trails and a restored barn with a cappuccino machine and a disabled toilet. Apparently there was flora, fauna and archaeology up here all along.

Today I was able to drive here and I should be able to hike to the summit in less than an hour and get back into the city centre in good time for my television recording. Both the beauty and the wind blow me away. The scenery is more weathered Celtic than pristine Alpine. I can imagine hordes of orcs from *The Lord of the Rings* marauding over this moorland rather than Julie Andrews and an ensemble of Von Trapps doing 'Do Re Mi'. As I climb there are few trees but I come across a hawthorn bush, no doubt saved for fear of the fairies, standing out all alone like a Belfast pacifist. It's an uncharacteristically sunny day but the wind is strong and persistent and it bends the mountain reeds around me to forty-five degrees. I stop at several streams, hopping over a sheugh to retrieve a shining sharp flint stone, wanting to believe this was once the arrowhead of a Neolithic hunter.

The mighty Divis transmitter still dominates the landscape like a base station on some lesser planet. As I gather pace I stumble across another sign, a rusting steel 'Give Way' signal inexplicably flapping in the wind at a junction of two mountain paths. Maybe I should detach the sign from this post and carry it down the mountain like a latter-day Presbyterian Moses. We could do worse than give way to one another a wee bit more in Belfast.

As I press on against the resistant winds a spectacular vista begins to unfold. Now I am standing adjacent to the Cavehill and across Belfast Lough I can see the more modest Holywood Hills. Nowadays Belfast is competing with their Californian namesake for international feature film production. They used to shoot people and dump their bodies on this mountain but today this is a place renowned for a different sort of shooting.

The view from the summit is breathtaking and I'm already out of breath. I look down on all of Belfast in wide-eyed wonder. Suddenly I am a boy again and the words that came to my mind when my only responsibility was to deliver forty-eight *Belfast Telegraph*s each night in the darkness come to me again. Class! Brilliant! Magic! Happy Days! I love this city.

There is a panoramic view across the whole of Northern Ireland and a distant ribbon of Scottish coastline. A glance at my phone reminds me of the time and a notification flashes across the screen warning me that I need to be sitting in a chair in a TV studio in Belfast city centre in less than an hour. A glimpse of the Isle of Man brings back memories of my first plane journey to a holiday to Douglas in 1970 when I paddled in the Irish Sea, tempting the waves to reach my shorts as I waded boldly into the icy surf.

Beyond the gentle drumlins of Down the mighty Mournes lurk like bullies, ready to pounce on poor wee Divis. It's almost exactly thirty years since I last stood here. The mountain hasn't changed but with all of Belfast laid out below me it's clear by how much the city has expanded. There are aeroplanes flying beneath me coming in to land at George Best City Airport and I can see the white stone of Stormont, a building whose proceedings have truly moved me only once, on the day of Geordie's funeral, when the city united in grief. The ferries to-ing and fro-ing on Belfast Lough now probably carry just as many immigrants from Eastern Europe as emigrants to England, in search of a decent living. Some familiar landmarks give me my bearings. The big yellow cranes of Samson and Goliath are a constant, although now a tourist destination for industrial archaeology rather than a working shipyard. The silvery glint of the prow-shaped roof of the Titanic Belfast Museum now competes for attention in

East Belfast. Scores of Victorian steeples endure, towering over declining congregations, and the City Hall dome is resplendent in the very centre of the city like a grand old lady surrounded by impudent adolescent skyscrapers. I can't see whether or not there's a flag flying on the City Hall; in fact I can see no flags at all from up here. Maybe flags don't really matter in the bigger picture. From up here the houses are neither orange nor green and their inhabitants are just tiny ants doing their best to stay alive and feed their young.

As I focus on the streets where I grew up I'm thrilled to spot Woodvale Park where I played on the swings and where trees are still carved with the words 'Tony loves Sharon. True.' From up here the beautiful little park is like a soaked green sod slapped amid the red-brick streets. As I follow the landmarks from Shankill to Falls it's clear that all the military installations have disappeared in the past thirty years as permanently as the hairs have disappeared from the top of my head. But a deep sadness overwhelms me when I see all too clearly what I already know: the peace walls separating republican and loyalist neighbourhoods are still with us. Built as a 'temporary measure' at the outset of the conflict in 1969 they have now outlived the Troubles and persist as a great steel security blanket because of the ingrained mistrust of succeeding generations. There is a glimmer of hope in that the peace walls seem smaller now, dwarfed by the urban spread and the massive city centre developments. But the areas where the peace walls remain are the poorest communities with the least investment and fewest opportunities for young people. Most people in Northern Ireland don't seem to care if the walls never come down – after all they don't affect them. But the peace lines are still visible from up here, like painful varicose veins affecting the city's arteries, keeping good people divided and impoverished and guaranteeing that ethnic bloc-voting remains intact.

Looking to the north of the city where I lived and worked in the later part of the 1980s I trace the Antrim Road from the renovated steeple at Carlisle Circus and notice a crisscross of fences in Clifton Park Avenue and the vacant site of Girdwood Barracks, the controversial former army site that is still being fought over by both sides. I try to spot the little house on the peace line where we lived from 1986 until 1988. Those were the years when I first attempted to put my pacifist principles into action. This was the time I decided to work for reconciliation across peace walls they were still building. When I was twenty-two years old we took a radical step. I haven't done many remarkable things in my life but this was certainly unusual, some would say crazy. I chose to live on the other side, in enemy territory, and to bring together young people from both sides. For a moment I forget that I'm late. My mind returns to Belfast 1986. As newlyweds, Lesley and I started out in that wee speck down there, in that tiny red-brick house on the peace line. Feelings of fear and excitement return. We were two young Presbyterians in love and choosing to live on the Catholic side of the peace wall to help bring an end to the killing. You really had to watch yourself round there. It could change very fast. But it's an experience that changed my life and a choice I will never regret. I could stand up here for hours just remembering it. Or I could go home and write it all down. Standing on top of Divis Mountain I resolve to share one of the many untold stories of the Troubles – the stories of ordinary people that will never make it in to the history books. I am going to write about the time when we lived in the little house on the peace line.

1

THE SUMMER OF '85

In 1985, I went to live on the other side of the peace line. Everyone said my head was cut. It was the summer of Live Aid and Bob Geldof pledged to save Africa from hunger. My ambitions were more modest. I wanted to stop fighting between Catholics and Protestants in Belfast.

In June of that year I started working as a volunteer for a new Christian charity, The 174 Trust. Our mission was to transform 174 Antrim Road into a drop-in centre for the people who lived in one of the most neglected and violent parts of Belfast. The youth unemployment rate was 90 per cent and the area had the highest concentration of sectarian killings in Northern Ireland. So many people had died on the streets here that the area was known as 'Murder Mile'.

The 174 Trust was set up by a few of the Protestant churches on the Lower Antrim Road. These churches found themselves in a mainly Catholic area due to the changing sectarian demographics of Belfast. The familiar pattern across the city was one side moving out and the other side moving in, which was just what had happened here. Most Protestant churches that found themselves in the same position at the time lingered on, hoping that their buildings would avoid becoming carpet showrooms for Catholics. But in this area of North Belfast some of the church leaders were talking about an exciting new concept called 'inner city ministry'. It was a model of outreach that was just as concerned about people's social needs as their spiritual state. This was my kind of faith. As I emerged from childhood my Jesus was steadily becoming less Billy Graham and more Martin Luther King, and not very Ulster Presbyterian at all. Churches obsessed with flowers, roof repairs and organs turned me off. I was attracted to believers with a passion for peace, justice and the poor.

So, to make myself useful, I volunteered to help clearing out the charity's premises, which were located where the New Lodge Road meets the Antrim Road, and where Catholics rarely meet Protestants. I was warned repeatedly that it was dangerous for a Protestant from the top of the Shankill Road to be doing youth work on the streets in an IRA stronghold. Looking back my fearlessness disturbs me – and I knew there was much to fear in North Belfast. The embattled population had already endured years of riots, bombs, shootings, abductions, torture and bodies dumped in the Belfast Hills. This was a place where terror had become normal. For many people from my background God was an angry old Orangeman waving his finger at them from the heavens like some giant cosmic Paisley. My God was gentle, compassionate, forgiving and wanted an end to violence, poverty and inequality. Driven by this belief, I suppressed my fear and took the road less travelled by, in the hope that it would make a difference. I dismissed the misgivings of others and, along with a group of similarly minded volunteers from different parts of Northern Ireland, England and the USA, I followed my convictions.

In July our crew of student volunteers redirected our focus from manual work on the old building to youth work on the streets. While the traditional summer riots raged around us and as the fighting over parades in Portadown exploded, we ran summer scheme activities every day for hundreds of children and young people in Duncairn Presbyterian Church Hall. We ran the children's club in the mornings and the teenager club in the evenings. One day it was games, Bible stories and a trip to the seaside and the next it was arts and crafts, quizzes and a barbecue in the forest. It was tough when someone stole the footballs or broke the windows but it was great craic nonetheless. I valued the warm camaraderie amongst the volunteers and I loved meeting the young people, even the ones that called me a speccy good-livin' bastard.

As a result of the exodus of Protestants from the Lower Antrim Road, most of the young people on the summer scheme were from the other side, while most of the volunteer youth workers were from our side. This was very unusual because even when it came to evangelism in Belfast you tended to stick with your own. Why would you want to stop your enemy from going to hell?

For as long as I could remember I had been sick and tired of all the talk of sides in this city. Everyone knew how to work out what side you were from in the first two minutes of meeting you.

'What's your name?'

'Where do you come from?'

'What school did you go to?'

'What team do you support?'

I didn't care what side you were from as long you didn't want to hurt anyone from the other side. The youngest children on our summer scheme were oblivious to sides and I loved their innocence.

When the summer scheme ended and the kids were getting ready to go back to school, I helped with the continuing renovations of the three-storey terrace at 174 Antrim Road, removing dead pigeons and several years of their shit from the staircases, painting fresh white gloss on skirting boards and scraping woodchip wallpaper from walls in the flats above the ground-floor shop unit.

We had been using the old shop unit as a makeshift café and youth club venue for a while now but once the latest renovations were completed the Saltshaker café and drop-in centre were re-opened. At first only a few people ventured in and there was some suspicion that we were a cult. But gradually local people who were curious about what 'them Christians' were up to dropped in and when they discovered that they would not be preached at over their Ulster Fry, more local residents began to discover that the centre was a warm and friendly gathering place. As part of my summer volunteering I put on an apron, prepared fried eggs and soda bread and microwaved burgers in the kitchen and served cups of tea to our new customers. I felt self-conscious that I was obviously not from round here and had Protestant written all over me. Some people didn't seem mind.

'You're a lovely big fella, so you are,' commented some of the pensioners.

Others were clearly trying to work out if I was a threat.

'Are you a fuckin' Hun?' enquired a few of the teenagers.

September came and, except for one unsuccessful application to Co-operation North, there was no sign of a job for me and I was starting to get worried. Earlier in the summer I had graduated from the University of Ulster at Coleraine with a BA Honours Degree in Media Studies. I was the first person in my family ever to get a degree. My mother and father had beamed with pride as my name was called to step forward to receive my degree from the Vice Chancellor. This was family history and the result of all their years of hard work and sacrifice to make sure their son got a good education no matter what. Graduation day was a welcome relief from the depression that seemed to have engulfed my parents while I was away at university. In their eyes I was the sole graduate in the class of '85. After the ceremony they cried and hugged me over the strawberries and cream. It was as if I had passed a thousand eleven-pluses. My professor shook my father's hand nervously with an uncharacteristic awkwardness that confirmed my long-held suspicions that he was more comfortable lecturing about the plight of the working man than speaking to one. We queued for a photographer who charged us almost as much as my father earned in a week at the foundry. I stood proudly in my new suit from Man at C&A, clutching a scroll and trying to look clever. But beneath the mortarboard and my well gelled mullet lurked the knowledge that I had been rejected from the media courses I had applied for in Dublin and Belfast, and that the BBC had turned me down as a newsreader after an ill-fated screen test when I had mispronounced half the locations in Ulster.

I needed a start. At the foundry where my parents worked, young people who left school with no qualifications used to ask for 'a start' and my father, who was a foreman, used to be able to sort them out. In fact he once got a death threat wrapped in a bullet for giving a start to a Catholic. But nowadays there was more talk of redundancies and lay-offs. My father was living in dread of a sudden announcement that the whole foundry would close down and he would lose the job he had worked at since he was sixteen years old. I couldn't imagine the whole of Mackie's closing down but I knew it was struggling to compete with companies in other parts of the world. Anyway, they didn't need any Media Studies graduates, so I had to look in other directions.

By late September I was signing on the dole in the Snugville Street unemployment bureau alongside everyone else on the Shankill Road. My academic prowess counted for nothing. I couldn't get a job without experience and I couldn't get experience without a job. My university days were a happily-ended story and this felt like the hard cold start of the first chapter of a darker book. Up until this time in my life everything I had tried my best to do had been a success. My experience was that if you worked hard you would do well. At first I was confident that by the end of my summer of volunteering for peace I would find a job. But three months after graduating and a series of failed applications I was beginning to have doubts.

At least my personal life was happy. I was engaged to Lesley. We had met at university and fallen in love over endless cups of coffee and late night conversations about everything and nothing. I had persuaded the bank manager to grant me an overdraft facility specifically so that I could buy Lesley a Princess Diana engagement ring.

I had volunteered in the summer schemes every year since I had left school and Lesley had joined me for the past two years. The children loved Lesley's enthusiasm and lively personality almost as much as I did and found her country accent just as different and funny as those of the American volunteers. The older teenagers were aghast at our chaste relationship. On one quizzing about our lack of sex life, on the way home in the minibus from a seaside barbecue in Drain's Bay, Big Mickey was incredulous when I confessed that we were waiting until we were married.

'Wise up, mister, you're a fuckin' liar,' he said.

'Or nat near wise in the head!' contributed Den.

'Or a wanker, as well as a speccy bastard,' added Tonto.

I assured them I certainly wasn't a liar.

Lesley was a fellow graduate of the class of '85 but she was back home up the country now and living with her parents again in Bellaghy. She had just been offered a place on a prestigious postgraduate Management Scheme in Belfast. The interviewers had obviously been impressed with her engaging personality and good business sense. I was delighted but Lesley's success only added to the pressure I was feeling. Hopefully she would stick by me and get married 'for poorer' for a little while in the hope I might at some stage manage 'for richer'. If I ever lost confidence Lesley put me right.

'You've no idea, wee lad,' she said. 'You've got potential.'

These supportive words told me all I needed to know – Lesley believed in me.

It had also been harder than I expected to move back home. My parents were still working in Mackie's, my mother in the wages office and my father in the foundry. My younger brother, Barry, was often at rugby practice after school at Belfast Royal Academy, following in his two brothers' footsteps (the school not the rugby, in my case). Terry my older brother was married now and had got a good job in Shorts and moved to Bangor. Yes, the three Macaulay brothers' names were Terry, Tony and Barry. Lesley referred to us a Huey, Dewey and Louie.

It was strange to be back home in my childhood bedroom after three years away in freezing student digs in Portstewart. The walls were still bereft of the posters I had removed when I had moved out but there were still a few bits and pieces around me from my childhood. Alongside my piles of *Guardian* newspapers, academic books, classic novels and Bible commentaries lurked a remote control Dalek and the *Whizzer & Chips Annual 1976*. My room felt familiar and comfortable but living with my parents at the age of twenty-two was a backward step. I was used to living with my peers who were full of craic and energy but returning home I found that both my parents were on anti-depressants. The strains of the Troubles along with a lack of job security seemed to have drained much of the joy from their lives.

Since I last lived at home both my mother's parents had passed away. My grandfather died suddenly after setting fire to his bed while smoking. My grandmother's insistence on staying in her own home and her constant demands became overwhelming, and, after one particularly stormy argument, my mother had a nervous breakdown. My father had been drinking heavily at home for several years now and was little support to my mother. When it became clear that my grandmother needed professional care she was moved into the Salvation Army Nursing Home and after a few months she died there. My mother's depression deepened and my father's guilt for not supporting her increased. The day my mother was admitted to the psychiatric hospital, my father poured every bottle of alcohol in our house down the drain. He never drank again, but descended into his own depression. I felt helpless. I wanted to make them better but I didn't know how. When I moved home I tried to cheer them up but I had my own life too and sometimes I felt guilty for just wanting to get away from all the gloom. I didn't want to end up middle-aged and miserable like them and I was already feeling more despondent by the day. Naively I concluded that the best thing I could do was to get a job that would make them proud so they would know that all their sacrifices for my education had not been in vain.

So when the 174 Trust advertised the position of director I applied straight away. Not long after, a letter arrived in the post. As I tentatively unfolded the paper I spotted the logo of The 174 Trust at the top of the page. The Reverend Patton Taylor, a red-haired Presbyterian minister from Scotland, had signed the letter personally in blue ink. As a result of his radical views on the church actually daring to help poor people in the inner city Rev. Taylor was the founding Chairman of the Trust. I read his typed words excitedly.

Dear Tony,
Thank you for your application for the post of Director of the 174

Trust. We would like to invite you for an interview …

I phoned Lesley straight away.

'I've got an interview!' I shouted.

Lesley gave one of her finest Bellaghy whoops of excitement.

The next week I attended the interview. A few days later I received a letter telling me I hadn't got the job as it had been offered to a forty-year-old Baptist pastor from Wales called John Evans, but tantalisingly inviting me to a second interview. After this interview with the Board of Trustees I was offered the job of Assistant Director of the 174 Trust, on the condition that I moved to live in the local community. And so in a matter of weeks I had to make the move from the Shankill to the New Lodge. While the distance between the two areas was short, the difference between them was vast. I would have to live on the other side of the peace line. I knew that for most people in Belfast such a move was pure madness. I had hardly been born with a silver spoon in my mouth, but the level of poverty and alienation from the state in the New Lodge was on a different scale to any I had previously experienced. It was one thing to volunteer for a few weeks every summer, but now I was going to live and work here every day. I was determined to reach across the barriers that divided my city – that idealism was soon to be shaken.

2

MOVING TO THE OTHER SIDE

It was good to have a job but bad to be without a home. I started work in four weeks and a condition of my employment was that I had to live within one square mile of the Saltshaker Centre at 174 Antrim Road. The Rev. Taylor summed up the reason behind this principle perfectly: 'We want to be a part of the local community, not a bunch of do-gooders from suburbia.' I agreed, although I was a do-gooder from up the Shankill, which was steadfastly non-suburban.

I respected Rev. Taylor because he practised what he preached, which was rare in Belfast. He lived with his wife and three small children in the old manse in the grounds of Duncairn Presbyterian Church. This church residence made the young family the most obvious of the few Protestants remaining on the Lower Antrim Road, which was now a republican area. The other few elderly Protestants in the nearby streets who had chosen not to move out tried to avoid unwanted attention by keeping their heads down. The manse had steel security grilles on the downstairs windows due to multiple burglaries. Sometimes Rev. Taylor typed his sermons on the floor of his office when there was shooting outside.

Upstairs, the cots in the children's bedrooms were situated well away from the windows to protect them from bullets or broken glass. Stone-throwing to break the Protestant windows of the manse was an acceptable youth sport – the RUC rarely caught the attackers but, of course, they had other priorities in the area at the time, such as recruiting informers and trying not to get shot. Other Protestant clergymen who had found themselves in similar circumstances had insisted on moving to safer areas, away from the social problems of their parishes. I respected the Taylors' courage in staying put.

Finding an affordable and available home for myself proved much more difficult than I had expected. My first port of call was the Northern Ireland Housing Executive on the Shankill Road. I queued for several hours in a dirty office that made the Snugville Street dole office seem palatial. I was certain that my meagre salary of £5,000 per year would entitle me to a council house. When I finally got to speak to a housing officer and enquired if I could live as close to the peace line as possible the housing officer's bright red plastic spectacles slipped down her well made-up nose in surprise and she raised her pencilled eyebrows ever higher. When I added that I wanted to live on the Catholic side her expression changed from surprise to that mix of concern that crosses a professional's face when it dawns on them that the person they are dealing with may be unhinged. I noticed her eyeing the panic button. She dispatched me with the news that as a single and employed person I wouldn't earn enough points to place me sufficiently high on the waiting list to get a house, in any area of Belfast.

My next tactic was to scour the classified advertisements in the *Belfast Telegraph*. The 'To Rent' section was always smaller than 'Deaths' and occasionally even had fewer columns than 'Pets' Corner' but I still studied the listings. Most of the rentals were in the once-fine Victorian terraces around the Antrim Road that had been crudely converted into flats when their middle-class inhabitants had scarpered as a result of the Troubles. Every single flat I viewed was cold and dirty with peeling woodchip wallpaper and evidence of mice. The worst smelt of boke and piss and there was a distinct whiff of marijuana seeping under the neighbours' flimsy doors. Even if these properties had been habitable, I was shocked to realise that I could not afford the rent. It seemed that most of these rents were paid for through housing benefit – they were more affordable on no pay than low pay. Then I spotted a room to let in a big old Victorian detached house off the Cavehill Road for an attractively low rent. When I arrived for the viewing the son of the elderly lady who was living out her days alone in this family home greeted me. It was a lovely old-fashioned house with wooden panels in the hallway and doilies on the arms of the sofas. The house felt warm and homely and the elderly woman seemed very nice, although a tad wary of me. Her devoted son explained to me that the reason for the low rent was that I would be expected to 'keep a wee eye' on his mother. After the viewing he explained the proposed arrangement to me in detail as he walked towards his BMW. As long as I was there in the evenings and every night I would be a suitable tenant, because there was a home help who visited his mother during the day. I wanted to tell him to look after his own mother, but I was still too polite to speak my mind and instead I phoned him later to explain it wasn't quite what I was looking for. However by this stage I was getting so desperate I had seriously considered accepting the role of night nurse just to secure a place to live.

Two weeks before I started the job – on the sort of sunny, bright September morning that scundered Belfast schoolchildren back at school after the long wet summer break – I went to meet my new boss, who had outperformed me at my first interview for the director post, and to see the office where I would be based. The Saltshaker Café was full of pensioners having cups of tea and scones and several burly workmen tackling mammoth Ulster Frys. The freshly painted walls, newly varnished second-hand chairs and sturdy pub tables made the Saltshaker look like a proper café. The only difference was the noticeboard for youth and community clubs and the carefully chosen gospel tracts that weren't about the unsaved going to hell or anything else offensive. The volunteers in the kitchen waved to me but they were too busy to chat as there was an altercation at the till with Tonto, a tall ginger teenager, who was protesting that he had not put his hand in the till and swiped a fiver when the volunteers' backs were turned to make him a cheese and ham toastie.

'I'm tellin' the fuckin' truth,' he protested. 'Yousens are supposed to be Christians and you don't even believe me.'

Tonto's flushed face belied his protestations of innocence.

'I'm John Evans,' said the newly appointed director in a soft Welsh accent that seemed out of place at the top of the New Lodge Road. It dawned on me that Lesley and my new boss shared a surname, and that I would be taking daily instructions from Evanses for the foreseeable future. John Evans was a small man in his early forties with a UDR moustache and a warm smile, and he seemed very down to earth for a Baptist pastor. He also had a twinkle in his eyes that suggested he wasn't all holiness. As soon as we met I understood why he had been chosen over me to lead the organisation – it was obvious that his experience and maturity outweighed mine.

'Shall we see upstairs?' he said, ushering me out the front door of the café to the adjacent large green door that led to the office and flats above. As Tonto ran past us with a box of Tayto cheese and onion crisps under his arm, he shouted, 'See! The Brits are even watching the Christians.' He was referring to the soldier who I could just about make out through the slits in the concrete and steel in the small, fortified army post that was on the other side of the café. It was a raised narrow concrete box in a massive steel cage, and the scorch marks from blast bombs and the accompanying graffiti made it clear that the Brits were not welcome here.

As we entered 174 Antrim Road I noticed fresh boot marks on the big green door. 'Don't worry – it's a very sturdy door,' said John.

We climbed the steep stairs to the office and when I looked back I noticed the heavy security bolts on the inside of the door and the steel grilles on the window at the top of the stairs.

'This will be your office,' said John, showing me into a room with old-fashioned woodchip wallpaper and two big windows overlooking the pub and the bookies across the main Antrim Road.

'We use this room for staff meetings and prayer meetings,'

explained John, pointing to the recently donated second-hand sofa and faded armchairs gathered around the fireplace, 'but there will be enough room at this end for a desk so it can be your office too.'

I nodded, imagining my pens and files and a stapler on my very first work desk. The floor vibrated as a bus passed by on the Antrim Road. This had previously been a flat – we were in the former living room, the main office was in the master bedroom, also overlooking the bookies on the Antrim Road, and the director's office was in the smaller bedroom at the back with security grilles on the windows. As John showed me around I found that the flat also contained a large kitchen with no appliances apart from a dirty sink with greasy taps, a broken oven and a lime-scaled kettle. The carpets in the hall were ancient and dirty but John and I agreed that the smell wasn't too bad and part of the sacrifice of full-time Christian service was making do with limited resources and a certain amount of hardship. At the back of the flat, beside the security door at the fire escape, there was a separate toilet and a bathroom with a small wash hand basin and a yellowing bath.

'The immersion heater still works so we always have hot water for the office,' explained John, as positively as possible.

It was at this moment that I had a brilliant idea, or maybe God spoke to me, or maybe both. The only thing missing was a bedroom, but if I could find a cheap sofa bed it could double up as somewhere for me to sleep at night and seating for the prayer meeting by day. I put the idea to John. He looked a little surprised. He never said the words but I noticed that his brow furrowed and his eyes twinkled in a manner that suggested he thought I was mad for wanting to live in a dump like this, beside an IRA-targeted British watchtower. John had been excused from living in the area because he had children. I thought this was unfair because I was given no option, and after all Rev. Taylor had young children and he lived here.

John said he had to check with the chairman but to my great relief Rev. Taylor accepted my suggestions and even agreed a low rent for the bedsit to be deducted from my monthly salary. I thought this was a generous arrangement, but when I told my father, he called Rev. Taylor a 'tight Scottish chancer' for asking me to pay any rent at all. 'If they can get you to believe all them fairy stories in the Bible, no wonder they can get you to agree to anything,' he said.

I did not listen to my father. I listened to my conscience, to God and to Rev. Taylor. I was overwhelmed with relief to have found somewhere that I could live until my wedding day in December the following year.

The next two weeks were hectic. I had to purchase all of the basic equipment to make my semi-bedsit semi-habitable. My most important investment was a sofa bed. Unfortunately my paltry resources did not stretch to the luxury of an actual sofa with a foldable bed frame. However I managed to source a bargain in the Texas Homecare slightly soiled section for £25. This sofa bed was basically three large pieces of foam covered in beige polyester that folded together to make a two-seater sofa. With minimal effort this lightweight material unfolded into a perfect single bed.

I claimed an old fridge that had been donated to the 174 Trust and I bought a two-ring tabletop cooker for £30 in the bomb-damage sale in the Co-op Superstore. A copy of *Cooking for One* by Delia Smith, a gift from my former P5 schoolteacher Ruth, completed my kitchen. Ten pounds worth of cleaning products upgraded the bathroom suite to almost white. I claimed some remnants from my parents' new hall and stairs carpet and a few old rugs from their roof space to cover all of the bare floorboards. For less than one hundred pounds I had created a bachelor pad.

Finally, I packed my clothes into both my parents' suitcases and all my favourite books and cassettes into several large boxes I'd found at Crazy Prices. I loaded everything into my father's Fiat Panda and transported my whole life two miles to the other side. I parked the car on the pavement to unload. I wondered if the soldiers inside the watchtower were discussing whether I was moving ammunition right under their noses, hidden beneath Abba's *Greatest Hits Volume 2*, *The Lord of the Rings* and a large red edition of *New International Version of the Bible*.

'You movin' in?' asked Soup en route to the bookies across the road.

'Aye,' I replied proudly.

'Fuckin' mental. Wait 'til you see what them bastards do to us round here,' he shouted, as a heavily armoured RUC Land Rover drove past.

I knew Lesley was calling soon and I wanted the bedsit to look impressive. I popped across the road to the wee shop and bought tea and coffee, a carton of milk, a Vienna roll, a tub of Flora and two apple turnovers.

BRRRRRRRRRRRRRRRZZZZ.

I ran down the steep flight of stairs to welcome Lesley but found instead Seamus and Antony, looking high and smelling of glue. I didn't know the brothers very well but they had a reputation for being hard men and I had been warned that Seamus was known to head-butt anyone who irritated him, including youth leaders. Seamus pushed his face right into mine, so close I that I inhaled some solvent. But he said nothing.

'Hi lads, what about ye?' I said calmly. 'I've just moved in.'

Seamus stared at me without blinking, still right in my face, while a girl pushing a pram distracted Antony.

'Ya wee hoor,' Antony called after the young woman, whose pace quickened notably.

'Are youse comin' to the youth club the marra night, lads?' I asked.

Seamus looked into my eyes intently but said nothing. I was hoping Lesley would arrive soon to save me. While I often felt in real fear of being walloped, Lesley could wrap lads like Seamus and Antony around her finger with a lovely smile and a hint of a double entendre.

"Mon you!' said Antony sadly and the brothers departed without either an assault or a farewell.

As they disappeared into the distance Lesley arrived in the Renault 5.

'The traffic!' said Lesley. 'You've no idea!'

As Lesley stepped out of the hatchback she instantly became the best-dressed person within a three-mile radius. Her obsession with fashion made her stand out from the crowd anywhere but especially here. I was afraid this would draw attention to us and I just wanted to blend in. The more people who noticed I was here the higher the possibility they would work out I was a Protestant living on the wrong side. Lesley knew she looked different but was not the kind of person who would change her clothes just because someone might think she didn't belong. I think she was braver than me. She was carrying a spider plant and a bottle of Domestos as my housewarming gifts.

'This place will need a woman's touch,' she proclaimed.

'Touch away,' I flirted.

As we made our way into the flat Patsy's mother was passing.

'Hello,' I said.

'Och hello, love,' she replied. 'Our Patsy loves your wee clubs so she does!'

'Tell Patsy it starts again the marra night,' I answered cheerfully. 'I'm just movin' in.'

Patsy's mother stopped for a second and turned around. 'Could you not find anywhere to live on your own side?' she asked.

There was an embarrassing pause and then I replied. 'I don't believe in sides.'

Patsy's mother laughed, more at me than with me, and walked on, as I ushered Lesley up to the flat. Lesley walked around my new accommodation.

'It's … um … lovely,' she said eventually.

'Do you wanna cuppa tea and an apple turnover?'

Lesley did not reply but immediately set to applying most of the contents of the bottle of Domestos to every conceivable corner in the kitchen. Once she was satisfied we settled down for a cup of tea in front of *Cagney & Lacey* on my ageing black-and-white television. At last I felt I had my own home. Of course it wasn't perfect, but my expectations had fallen as my search for accommodation had become more desperate. Although I would only be living here for a short period I felt proud of myself for choosing some hardship and sacrifice in my life like a missionary living in a hut in Africa. When Lesley departed with a goodnight kiss she commended my efforts on making the bedsit habitable and for making the best of a pig's ear. But I knew that there was no way Lesley could have lived here. She had grown up in a big house in the country with outhouses and an orchard and this tiny flat was smaller than the stable for her ponies.

I didn't sleep well on my first night. I had to get used to the normal creaks and bangs of the building, which I mistook for rats and robbers. The 6 a.m. bus to Glengormley created a shudder that vibrated across the floorboards and rattled the windows like a minor quake. I got up early to start work, folded my bed and looked across the room. I was already at work. My daily commute would consist of three steps from my bed to my desk.

When the small staff team arrived we gathered on the sofas in my room for the prayer meeting. John Evans arrived a little late as he was sorting out an incident of alleged theft by one of our painters and decorators on the Action for Community Employment (ACE) Scheme. The complainant did not regard our young worker as ace in any way. As a result of his late arrival John had to sit on the new sofa bed, which although comfortable as a bed was not a very supportive sofa and he lost some of his dignity leading us in a prayer for the lost souls of North Belfast while sinking into the sofa foam so rapidly that his knees were at a higher level than his head. After the Amen I was introduced to my new colleagues, some of whom I knew from volunteering on past summer schemes; Stewart who ran the café and the junior youth clubs along with Eleanor (a church volunteer from England), Jean who visited the local senior citizens and ran the pensioners' club and Joan who was the secretary and fount of knowledge on all that was going on inside and outside of the office. Next I had to pop around the corner, past the army watchtower and the church, for a meeting with Rev. Taylor in the Manse. As I walked around the corner I bumped into Gerry looking bleary-eyed.

'I've to sign on in Corporation Street,' he sniffed. 'I hate them oul' dolls down there. They treat us like shite.'

'Are you coming to the youth club the night in the Saltshaker?'

Gerry drew deeply on his cigarette. 'Aye, maybe. I hear you're livin' round there nigh?'

'I moved in yesterday.'

'Is big Lesley nat movin' in with ye?'

'No, Gerry, sure you know Christians wait 'til they're married, so we do.'

'I couldn't wait 'til I got to yer woman's house last night. I lumbered her up the entry.'

'Charming,' I replied.

'Anyway yousens livin' in them flats is the only Prods round here, apart from that ginger vicar and a few coffin dodgers round the corner. You need to watch yourself round here.'

'What's wrong with Protestants, Gerry?'

'No offence, mate. There are some good ones, but you can't really trust them.'

At this moment I was stunned to hear a North Belfast Catholic parrot the exact opposite of what I had heard a million times as a West Belfast Protestant. Somehow I had assumed that sectarianism was a peculiarly Protestant phenomenon because I had heard it articulated so many times by my own side. But I had never heard casual sectarianism expressed in such a similar words from the other side. This was different from people shouting at you in the street and calling you an Orange bastard. Most people in Belfast only voiced their sectarian feelings in front of their own sort. The IRA always insisted it was just unionists who were bigots and that republicans were entirely clean from political and religious hatred, a concept that must have been baffling for their victims as they shot them in the head. Gerry interrupted my reflections.

'Youse Christians are all right, like,' he said.

'Thanks Gerry,' I smiled. 'Being a Christian is more important than being a Catholic or a Prot ...'

Before I could finish, Gerry interrupted.

'But I'd still feed the whole bloody lot of youse to the fuckin' lions.'

3

THE LADS

BRRRRRRRRRRRRRRZZZZ!
BRRRRRRRRRRRRRRZZZZ!
BRRRRRRRRRRRRRRZZZZ!

The front door buzzer at 174 Antrim Road was already starting to get on my wick. It buzzed me first thing in the morning like an urban cock-a-doodle-do if any of my colleagues chose an early start to their day. Often it screeched throughout the night when mischievous youth club members or passing drunks pushed the button with the sole intention of disturbing me.

But this evening it was buzzing because the volunteers were arriving for the preparations and prayer meeting before the Tuesday night over-fourteens youth club. I was to be youth leader in charge, which was like being appointed head keeper at Belfast Zoo, but marginally more dangerous. This senior club was regarded as the toughest in the Saltshaker because the young people were generally uncontrollable but I enjoyed it the most of all the youth activities because I felt that it offered a real opportunity to get to know the young people, have decent conversations, and try to help them with their problems. This was the most violent square mile in the most violent part of the most violent city in Northern Ireland. The youth unemployment rate was 90 per cent. But I was determined that I would make a difference to these young people's lives. I wanted the Saltshaker to be the best youth club in Belfast, even if our resources were limited – five or six volunteers, a damaged pool table with missing balls and a box of broken board games. The aims of the youth club were to give the young people somewhere safe to go and something positive to do. The alternatives were underage drinking in the parks, getting involved in sectarian riots or hanging around the street corners, which were often targeted for drive-by shootings by the paramilitaries. Young people could drop in to the youth club between eight and ten every Tuesday night to play table tennis, pool or board games or just to have a chat with each other and the youth leaders over a snack from the tuck shop.

The voluntary youth leaders came from the local Baptist church, the summer team and the Christian Unions at Queen's and Jordanstown universities. Most young believers in Northern Ireland would have preferred a missionary posting to Africa to getting their hands dirty on these streets, so these volunteers were a special minority – courageous, committed and idealistic. Tonight's crew of Alan, Bill, Lois, Jamesy and Christine were among the most faithful and reliable.

I dashed down the stairs, darting off a quick prayer that I would do a good job on my first night as leader, that a good number of young people would turn up, that there would an opportunity to share the love of God and that loyalist paramilitaries would not target us for a drive-by shooting. This horrific possibility was always on my mind.

I opened the door with a smile. A tall ginger figure confronted me.

'Is it nat open yet?' asked Tonto.

'It's not open for another half hour, Tonto,' I replied.

'Fuck sake!' scowled Mo standing behind him.

'Won't be long,' I said, spotting the volunteers making their way through the group of around ten teenagers who were now standing at the front door of the Saltshaker waiting for the youth club to open.

'All right lads, calm down now, will ye?' implored Alan.

'Open it nigh, or we'll burn it down,' shouted Soup. 'Only sleggin', Tone,' and he winked.

'We just have to have a wee meeting and a quick prayer and we'll be down to open up,' I explained calmly, holding the door firmly with one hand and ushering in the volunteers.

Mo began to kick the steel security grilles on the front door.

'Them fuckin' Brits is spyin' on us,' complained Gerry, pointing to the army watchtower.

The commotion did appear to be gaining some attention from someone inside the security post, visible only through the steel slit as a pair of eyes.

'*Tiocfaidh ár lá*,' shouted Marty.

'Won't be long,' I said, wrestling the door closed and heading upstairs to the bedsit.

The volunteers sat down for a quick meeting, while the doorbell buzzed incessantly for a full half hour. After deciding who would do the door, who would monitor the pool tournament and who would keep an eye on the money and the tuck shop, we asked God to protect us, to give us patience and to help us to show Christian love to the young people of the youth club, no matter what the provocation.

'Yeeeeeooooooooo!' cried the group of impatient teenagers when we finally came downstairs to open up.

''Bout fuckin' time,' shouted Den, his eyes open unnaturally wide.

The youth club members spilled in through the door in a heaving mass of torn jeans, worn-out leather jackets and cigarettes in front of most of the volunteers. As a result, Tonto and Mo didn't pay their admission fee of 20p each and, in spite of repeated requests, managed to avoid settlement for the rest of the night.

Soup grabbed the fire extinguisher from the wall and jumped up on to one of the tables brandishing the spray tube like a weapon. 'I'm gonna empty this over the whole bloody lot of youse,' he shouted with glee.

'Scuffles!' echoed around the room.

They had heard the word 'scuffles' used by a posh English reporter on the BBC national news to describe a street disturbance that some of them had been involved in. They thought this was a ridiculous British choice of words and ever since had shouted 'scuffles' at the start of every fight.

'Come on now, Soup, stop messin'. If you do that you'll be barred,' I warned unconvincingly.

'Who gives a fuck?' shouted Soup, his eyes opening ever wider with excitement.

Soup was a good lad who had been dealt an unfair hand. He had been orphaned when a British army tank had crashed into his innocent parents, killing them both. Although I was only five years older than him, I felt fatherly towards him. In spite of the pain he had endured he had a good sense of humour and an infectious smile. Although he messed round as much as his mates I sensed I could trust Soup. Even though it would have been understandable for him to be bitter, he was not obsessed with violence or vengeance. Soup gave me hope. He deserved a better start in life than this city had given him. I wanted to do what I could to help him find some good opportunities in life. He spent too much time in the bookies and I wanted to help him to get some training and a decent job.

As Patsy and Colette ran in through the door without paying their 20ps, Soup thrust the tube of the fire extinguisher between his legs and shook it suggestively towards the girls.

'Wise up!' shouted Patsy. 'It's only as big as that in your dreams, wee lad.'

'Come on everyone, remember the youth club rules,' I said, attempting to assert some authority. 'No violence, no swearing and no damaging the equipment.'

Still brandishing the fire extinguisher, Soup shouted, 'I'll smash this over your fuckin' head,' breaking all three rules in one sentence.

'Fuck you up,' interjected Colette. 'Sure you suck dead dogs' dicks!'

'Girls, really,' said Lois, in an attempt to calm things down.

The girls and boys usually socialised separately in the youth club, but although the girls were always a minority, they were as fierce as any of the lads given cause.

A scuffle ensued.

'Scuffles!' shouted everyone.

It seemed my work was going to be cut out for me here as leader in charge of the uncontrollable. I never knew what to expect on a Tuesday night. Drink, drugs and the latest street violence made it very unpredictable. I worried that if it got completely out of control one of the young people or one of the youth leaders might be seriously assaulted. As Jamesy and Christine set to regaining control of the entrance, Lois managed access to the tuck shop and Alan took on supervision of the back room with the pool table, I continued negotiations with Soup. He finally climbed down for a smoke and admitted he had no intention of actually spraying the room with with the fire extinguisher.

'I just wanted to see your bake, Tone! I was only sleggin' and you were keekin' your breeks,' he laughed. 'It was class.'

In a bid to maintain some authority I tried to stifle a laugh. Soup was the sort of person that you liked instantly.

In a moment of calm, I invited Jeff and Michael, who had just arrived, to join me in a Connect 4 competition. Jeff was generally more sensible than most of his peers and unusually gentle for a teenage boy in North Belfast. He loved animals and was genuinely interested in God. Michael was blonde and handsome and keen to assert that he was the most intelligent member of the club.

I planned to let them win a few games, just to build up some rapport. Six consecutive defeats later along with the requisite taunts and celebrations I realised that such magnanimity would not be required. It did seem that Michael probably was the most intelligent, albeit the biggest slabber, in the youth club. A subsequent game between Tonto and Mo resulted in a fiery argument and both the yellow and red counters were fired across the room like stones at the Brits. I had never before considered the parts of a board game as lethal projectiles. In the crossfire I was struck in the eye by a red counter and my eyes watered as if I was crying.

'Dry your eyes, mister,' commented Colette.

'I'd deck him for doin' that!' exclaimed Gerry.

'What about turning the other cheek?' I asked.

'Wise up, wee lad!' said Gerry.

Just as I was about to challenge Gerry to a game of pool over which I hoped to get the chance to chat to him about why not retaliating might be the smarter choice, Billy arrived, smelling of drink.

'You know you're not allowed in if you've drink taken, Billy,' I told him.

Billy was only eighteen years old but he looked like he was in his late twenties. He had scars on his face from previous drink-fuelled fights and as a result of a few beatings from the Brits.

'I haven't touched a drop since the weekend,' said Billy.

Billy was the worst liar of all the youth club members. While Gerry could convince you that he hadn't really stolen Christine's guitar and sold it for cash in Smithfield Market, Billy's sad and honest eyes gave away every fib. Billy had two burdens to carry in life; one was having such a Protestant name in such a Catholic neighbourhood and the other, much more tragic, was the trauma of his father's horrific murder in a pub bombing at the start of the Troubles.

'They burnt him alive, the Orange bastards!' he would exclaim.

I was appalled when the young people described how British soldiers and police officers regularly taunted Billy about his father's murder. They knew what hurt him the most and then they used it to harass and torment him. Billy had recently taken to painting KAP, which stood for 'Kill All Prods', on the walls around the lower Antrim Road. While the watchful British soldiers were possibly investigating the emergence of a new republican paramilitary splinter group, I felt that it was just Billy missing his dad. His mother had done her best but he was stuck on the dole, trapped by the Troubles and drinking too much. I thought that if he had grown up in another place and another time he would have been a normal teenager. I broke the rules and let Billy in – he would be safer in here messing about with pool cues and threatening me than outside shouting obscenities at the British army.

'Aye, ya let him in when he's blootered,' complained Den, still bitter about being barred from the summer scheme for attempting to sniff a Lynx deodorant in the boys' toilets.

I patted Billy on the back and told him to behave himself or I would get into trouble with Rev. Taylor for allowing him into the youth club with alcohol on his breath. I returned to the back room where Gerry was waiting for a battle at the pool table. He beat me convincingly at the game, and we continued our debate about the rights and wrongs of the use of violence to achieve your political objectives.

'All this Christian shite's all right,' said Gerry, 'but this is war. Them Brits are killin' our people every fuckin' day. Do you expect us to just sit down and take it?'

'Well, they're gettin' killed too,' I argued. 'Are their lives not valuable too? Is it really worth taking even one human life over who runs a country?'

'The Brits have oppressed and murdered the Irish people for hundreds of years,' he said. 'There'll never be peace until the British are out of Ireland.'

'But how many people are you going to have to kill to achieve that?' I asked, 'What sort of Ireland would it be after all the killing?'

'It's war!' repeated Gerry.

I was soon to learn that this was the answer to everything. In war you could justify any violence you inflicted on the enemy, while at the same time burn with righteous anger at any attempt to justify the violence inflicted on your own side. Gerry proceeded to beat me three times and celebrated by raising his pool cue above his head like a victorious Zulu holding aloft his spear while chanting intermittently '*Tiocfaidh ár lá*' and 'Three nil, three nil, three nil …'

This was a typical Tuesday night in the senior youth club – an unpredictable mix of mayhem, aggression, petty theft, clunky evangelism, good conversation and great craic (usually at Big Mickey's expense). Mo stuck chewing gum in Patsy's hair and suffered a serious kick to his testicles as retribution; Flump threatened to rip Joe's arm off for nicking his cigarette lighter; Christine and Lois tried to explain the concept of Christian forgiveness to Colette; and everyone laughed at Big Mickey for hitting a reddener when Bernard revealed that Mickey's ma had found his porn magazines under the mattress in his bedroom.

That first night marked the first of the weekly sit-ins. These became my main fear during the youth club, second only to my nightmares about a gun or bomb attack on the premises. Three or four members of the club refused to leave at closing time and sat on the pool table with their arms folded, chanting 'sit in', 'scuffles' and 'up the 'RA'. After a long day at work followed by two hours on full alert during the club, the sit-in was guaranteed to test my patience to the limit, and the lads knew it.

'Come on, lads, you're really startin' to get on my bloody wick,' I growled, with scant remaining mercy or compassion.

'Yeoooooooo! You're nat so Christian nigh, so you're nat!' was the jubilant response.

Any attempt to remove the protestors would have ended in violence so we had to rely on talking therapies to solve the weekly drama. I sometimes wondered if this was good preparation for becoming a famous hostage negotiator like Terry Waite in the Middle East, but my failure in the back room of the youth club on the Antrim Road suggested that was not my vocation.

The 'sit in' that first night only ended after Big Mickey and Marty decided it was 'as borin' as fuck' and Soup wanted to get home in time to watch the snooker on TV. Once the exhausted youth leaders departed I finally locked the front door and padlocked the security grilles. As the last few youth club members loitered outside the Saltshaker under the watchful eye of the British army watchtower, an RUC police Land Rover sped past, the familiar dull grey paintwork on its armour-plated sides splattered with white paint.

'Yeeoooooooo,' shouted Tonto.

'We paint-bombed the black bastards last night,' boasted wide-eyed Den, 'for three hundred years of British oppression!'

'Come on, lads. I know you don't like the police, but they're only going to hassle you even more if you throw paint at them,' I said. 'Like, they're only trying to do their job.'

'Sure they're all fuckin' Huns,' scowled Gerry.

I was thinking of my cousins, my parents' neighbours and my old school friends who were police officers and who lived under constant threat of assassination by the IRA. To me the police were human beings, some of whom I knew personally, but to the lads in the youth club they were a harassing, discriminatory enemy to be resisted, attacked and killed. I wanted to be careful not to sound like I was taking sides but it was obvious that my experience and views of the police as benevolent keepers of law and order was out of place on this side of the peace line. I believed the young people when they told me how the police stopped and searched them for no reason but I assumed it was probably exaggerated to justify killing them. My thoughts of how to argue for peace without sounding like I was arguing for unionism were interrupted by the roar of the police Land Rover doing a sharp U-turn on the road and speeding back towards us. The back doors opened and an open tin of white paint was hurled in our direction. The paint just missed the teenagers and splattered all over the pavement. As the police sped off I could hear their jeers and laughter. Unaccustomed cheers in an English accent echoed in the British army watchtower.

'Ya see! Ya see!' shouted Den. 'You wouldn't believe they would do that, would ye?' He danced around the splattered paint pointing at it with glee. 'Look, look at that! Ya see! Ya see! Now do you believe us?'

'That's terrible,' I answered, genuinely shocked.

'Fuckin' black bastards,' shouted Mo, followed by a series of more 'fucks' than I had hitherto thought possible to accommodate in a single sentence.

'They shouldn't being doin' that,' I said.

'*Tiocfaidh ár lá*,' shouted Gerry.

Tonto fired a half-empty can of Lilt in the direction of the retreating Land Rover, but our friendly police patrol had disappeared at speed. The next most obvious target was the army and so the watchtower was attacked with bottles, stones and shouts of every conceivable foul name for a Brit.

'Take it easy, lads,' I said. 'They have guns in there.'

I may have been unaccustomed to being attacked by the police, but I was well aware of the dangers of a trigger-happy English teenager in a khaki uniform. The sudden transformation of my youth club members from mischievous and wild but likeable teenagers to young men filled with hatred shocked me, but this was my first direct experience of why the young people felt this way. They had grown up with this. Suddenly, from one of the side streets, an army Saracen arrived on the scene. The young people scarpered instantly and within seconds the only evidence of them ever having been there were distant shouts of '*Tiocfaidh ár lá*' from a far-off entry. I was left to retreat casually through the doorway of 174 Antrim Road in the hope that I would not be mistaken as the ringleader of an attack on the British army.

I had grown up assuming that the police only gave you hassle if you were up to something illegal and you deserved it. When nationalists accused the RUC of this sort of behaviour the unionist politicians denied that it ever happened and called it IRA propaganda. Of course, most Protestants privately admitted that there were dodgy policemen because they knew them personally, but these errant officers were always described as 'a few bad apples'. I had just seen with my own eyes a whole Land Rover full of bad apples. I was learning that on this side of the peace line the RUC were far from friendly bobbies. I always believed there were two sides to this conflict but I had only ever heard the other side's views expressed in words. For the first time I fully understood the saying 'never criticise a man until you've walked a mile in his moccasins'.

I firmly locked all the doors on my way back up to the flat and I thanked God for keeping us all alive and safe. I was happy that so many young people had turned up and enjoyed the youth club. I was glad to be building a little trust and respect, although worried that we were a target for an attack.

As I unfolded my sofa bed and got into my sleeping bag I could still smell gloss paint from the spots that had splashed on to my mullet. I lay very still in the darkness listening for evidence of broken windows, forced locks, guns loading and mice. I prayed for Billy, Soup, Den and Gerry, and even for Tonto. Living and working on the other side every day and night for the foreseeable future was clearly going to be an education and a challenge.

4

MAKING A DIFFERENCE

The constants of my new job were long prayers, longer working hours and a low salary. All I wanted to do was to make a difference: to prevent Gerry fighting on the streets, to get Den off the glue, to get Jeff on a training course and to help anyone get a job. I was trying to bring peace to Belfast one young person at a time, one street at a time but it was much harder than I had expected. I had to raise funds for a new pool table, make an insurance claim for the latest burglary, avoid getting a good beating and learn how to load an office stapler. I experienced the reality of jargon that was part of life in Belfast then, such as 'culture of violence' and 'deeply divided society.' The youth club members taught me the meaning of 'doing the double' and 'you haven't a fuckin' notion, wee lad'.

It was as clear as the peace line in Duncairn Gardens that I had an awful lot of work to do. My days began with early morning prayer meetings in the Manse, sometimes accompanied by fortifying porridge. Rev. Taylor seemed to believe that God listened more carefully to our prayers if we got up very early and presented them half asleep. After that, most of my mornings were filled with researching and writing funding applications and letters to every charitable trust and foundation I could find. If I were going to make a difference I would need greater resources. We struggled to pay the wages each month and most of the youth club equipment was old, broken or missing, due to theft. I was the one responsible for fundraising so I applied to each and every source that might be interested in giving money for peace or young people or faith-based community initiatives or Northern Ireland. As I developed my begging-letter-writing skills, my success rate gradually improved from one in thirty replying with a polite 'no' to one in twenty giving us a donation. Everyone from the Joseph Rowntree Foundation to Cliff Richard was tapped so that we could pay the wages, get a new table tennis table or fund a youth weekend away to the Mourne Mountains.

Every afternoon was different. Some days I would go to a training course at the Northern Ireland Council for Voluntary Action in Annadale Avenue and meet my peers from other voluntary organisations from all over Northern Ireland. During the tea breaks everyone would complain that the funding was drying up and that it was all the government's fault. On these courses I learned how to make a good funding application and how to write an eye-catching press release because the media generally ignored you if you weren't trying to kill anyone. On other afternoons I went to networking meetings with local youth and community groups from different parts of North Belfast that were organised by some of the citywide groups with a view to helping us to share information and work together. Cue more complaints about funding and the government. The more outspoken community workers made it clear that they felt that certain organisations did not represent their communities. It was clear that they regarded me as a representative of a wicked patriarchal charity that was being used as a pawn and a 'safe' way to funnel British government funding into areas of high social deprivation. Republican community workers called this 'political vetting' and I understood from the outrage that it was preventing IRA-controlled community groups from receiving grants from the British state. Politically and paramilitary aligned community workers in Belfast have never been renowned for their sense of irony, although their success in securing funding knows no bounds. I thought it was a good idea to give funding to voluntary groups that didn't support killing anyone but I said nothing and kept my head down. Meanwhile I experienced a wee taste of a different kind of vetting from the Northern Ireland Voluntary Trust.

'And do you try to convert the young people in the youth club?' asked the funding officer when I asked for money to buy a table tennis table.

I'd love to see me try, I thought.

'No,' I explained politely. 'It's a Christian social action project not an evangelistic mission.'

'But are you not forcing your religion on the young people?' continued the funding officer.

We're giving them somewhere to go and something to do and they just want a bloody table tennis table, I wanted to say. But I had to hide my exasperation because we really needed the money. My only motivation was to get some new recreational equipment for the young people but I had to work extra hard to reassure suspicious funders that I wasn't going to take their money and spend it all on gospel tracts or an air fare to bring Billy Graham over to run a tent mission on the New Lodge Road.

It was a new experience for me to be the only Protestant at so many of these community group meetings and I didn't feel particularly welcome. For most of my life I had been in the majority in social, religious and community gatherings. Most Belfast people prefer it that way. Sticking to your own is easy. I soon discovered that proper community workers were Catholic, atheist, socialist and nationalist. I spoke with a Belfast Royal Academy accent, which only confirmed the assumption that I was a middle-class do-gooder. I learned from more seasoned community workers that community development was all about doing only what the community wanted. I agreed with this but I noticed some men who had been community workers for years didn't bother asking their community and just put forward what they wanted. When I made the suggestion that working together on social issues across the community divide might have more impact than doing it separately I was challenged.

'My community does not want any of your so-called cross-community work that pretends that the problem here is sectarian-ism between Catholics and Protestants and not the presence of the British war machine in the six-county statelet,' explained a humourless community worker who had presumably consulted every single resident in his estate on the matter before making this pronouncement.

I was learning every day about how the British army was making the situation worse then better, but I desperately wanted to point out that most of the Catholic young people I worked alongside every day talked openly about hating 'all them Orange bastards' on the other side of the peace line. This seemed to me like the kind of ingrained sectarianism that wouldn't go away with the departure of the British army. Growing up on my side I had always despaired that so many people were against reaching out to the other side. It was a revelation to discover that it was pretty much the same on this side.

One morning John Evans informed me that we would be having a top-secret visit from a VIP that afternoon. Security would be very tight. John declined to divulge the name of the special guest but I assumed it was more likely to be Margaret Thatcher than Dirty Den from *Eastenders*. As the time of the visit approached and Joan, the charity's secretary, organised proper teacups and saucers and a few packets of Mr Kipling's cakes, the soldiers outside created a high-security exclusion zone around the Saltshaker Centre. When the visitor – who turned out to be Richard Needham MP, under-secretary of state for Northern Ireland – arrived he had several Saracen-loads of soldiers with rifles with him for protection. Very well for him, but I was concerned about when they all went home to England and left us open to possible attacks as punishment for hosting a British minister in a republican community. When he arrived he was ushered into John's office by several civil servants in suits while security men guarded the door and watched out the windows for snipers. I could feel my heart beating faster and faster. I was nervous that I might not be able to answer the MP's questions or that the Provos might try to bomb him for invading their territory or shoot us for allowing him to venture into our premises.

'We employ over fifty people in the ACE Scheme,' explained John politely. 'If local people have been unemployed for at least twelve months they are eligible for the scheme and we employ them for one year to work on various community projects.'

'Yeeeees,' said the VIP, 'and what sort of work do these chaps do?'

'We have a team of gardeners, and a team of painters and decorators, and we provide a free service to elderly and disabled people who need their gardens tidied up or their homes painted. It helps the unemployed and the elderly at the same time.'

Mildly impressed, the MP then turned to me. I did my best to explain our youth work in as positive a way as possible and with a minimums of ums and ahs. At the end of my presentation Richard Needham did not look at me directly or ask me any questions but he turned to his assistant and talked about me as if I wasn't in the room. It reminded me of the way English men in pith helmets talked about the natives in Tarzan movies, just before they got speared.

'Grammar school? Eh? Eleven-plus? Eh? That's where we're going wrong back home.'

I was disappointed that he seemed more interested in me as an example of the success of the Northern Ireland grammar school education system, which in fact failed most of the children where I came from, rather than in my attempts to address the problem of youth unemployment that his government had helped to create.

*

My days were sometimes made trickier when some familiar-looking young people wearing balaclavas were given permission by the republican leaders who had complete control in the community to hijack and burn a few buses, and to block the main road in the cause of a free Ireland, right outside the front door. Walking around smouldering vehicles was a great inconvenience to my busy work schedule. The best afternoons were in the drop-in centre when I was able to talk to the young people about their lives and to help them to sort out some of their problems. I got my eyes opened. We talked about God and contraception and how to get a job. We discussed drugs and politics, war and peace and sometimes had a confidential chat about problems with girlfriends or a violent da. One day Michael was distraught at getting his girlfriend pregnant and the next day Ed turned up homeless as his father had kicked him out of the house for taking drugs.

When it came to getting a job their sense of hopelessness was overwhelming. It was frustrating to see bright young people suffering from depression because they believed they would never work for the rest of their lives. I tried to reassure them that I believed one day they would have a good job and a decent living wage. In the short term at least we could offer some people a job on our ACE Scheme for a year.

One afternoon two of my youth club members, brothers Paddy and Joe, asked me to accompany them to their house to meet their older sister whom they had lived with since their parents had died. The British army had killed their mother, and their father had died of alcoholism caused by grief. The orphaned brothers seemed both lost and hardened as a result of their tragedy. They never had enough money for the latest fashions worn by their peers. A home visit was an unusual request, and I didn't really trust Paddy and Joe, so I was cautious. When we arrived at the house there was no sign of a sister but instead they proceeded to show me a 'replica gun' they kept in the house.

'Sure hold it, Tony,' they said encouragingly.

I declined to put my fingerprints on the weapon, just in case it was not a replica after all. I could not quite work out the motivation for this unusual home visit. It might have been a test to check if a British army raid on their house would follow, which would make it obvious that I was a tout, and we all knew what happened to touts. Perhaps it was an attempt to frame me by getting my fingerprints on a weapon. It wasn't until I returned to 174 and saw Mick pushing the Super Ser from the Saltshaker up the road that I suspected that they'd wanted me off site so that Mick could have a clear run at the centre. I ran to catch up with him but the faster I ran, the quicker Mick pushed the Super Ser. The gas fire looked like a demented R2D2 being stolen by a post-apocalyptic looter in *Mad Max* 3. Out of breath and sweating I finally arrived at Mick's flat. I rang the doorbell for a good half hour and when I spotted Mick peeking out through an upstairs window I shouted to him to return the heater. He didn't.

Of course, reporting this theft to the RUC was out of question, as this would have been regarded as a Protestant informing on a republican to the British state. The consequences of this were much worse than losing a gas heater. When I returned to the now freezing Saltshaker Centre the pensioners were complaining about the cold. I sat down exhausted and exasperated. Thankless wee bastards like Mick were taking me for a ride every day and I was exhausting myself in the process. I didn't take it personally because Mick's main income was through stolen goods but I felt let down because I had tried to help him. Mick was clearly quite capable of helping himself. It sometimes felt as if I was making no difference whatsoever.

At least Lesley's career was going from strength to strength. She was completing her postgraduate management course and getting job placements with private sector companies with yuppies and Filofaxes in a Belfast city centre that seemed light years away – rather than just one mile – from the Lower Antrim Road.

We had agreed that the wedding would take place the following year, just after Christmas. My future mother-in-law deemed the Country House Hotel in Kells the top place for the perfect rural Ulster wedding reception and so it had been booked for 27 December 1986. We had just over a year for Lesley to find a job and for us to find our first home together, which – as stipulated in my contract – had to be within one square mile of 174 Antrim Road. I knew from my attempts at finding a flat to rent that our house search was not going to be easy, but at least we had time on our side. In the meantime Lesley was sharing a house in East Belfast with Jennifer, a friend from the Presbyterian Church in Bellaghy who was also working in Belfast. We were happy and excited as we looked toward the Big Day.

However, my parents' depression was getting worse. I had just as many family issues as half the young people in the youth club. My father had stopped drinking after my mother's nervous breakdown but now he was clinically depressed too. 'You'll end up in Purdysburn' was a jokey Belfast phrase to indicate that some circumstance might drive you mad. Believe me, it was no joke when both your parents were in Purdysburn with clinical depression at the same time. As I tried to support other people through hard times in their lives at the 174 Trust I was trying to come to terms with the mental illness that was devastating my own family. Little did my colleagues and youth club members know that behind my cheerful and positive exterior I was trying to cope with the trauma of my father's post-alcohol withdrawal symptoms and the horror of my mother's electric shock therapy.

When I wasn't spending my evenings at Purdysburn I put in a lot of time at the various youth clubs. At the weekends I went on 'deputation' visits to churches across Northern Ireland to seek prayers and donations to keep our work going in North Belfast. Many of these congregations seemed fascinated and inspired by our groundbreaking urban mission work but usually their donations barely covered the cost of my petrol.

I was working too hard, not getting enough sleep and not taking breaks for meals, thanks both to the limited kitchen facilities in the bedsit and the allure of Manny's fish & chip shop up the road. I ended up having to visit the doctor who referred me to the Royal Victoria Hospital for an investigative procedure to check my stomach for an ulcer. This involved anaesthetising my gag reflex and inserting a newfangled tube with a camera down my throat to broadcast live pictures of my intestines to the consultant. On my doctor's advice and at Lesley's insistence I decided to take my lunch break, eat more healthily and take some time off work for other interests and hobbies. I rekindled my lifelong obsession with science fiction and bought a model Dalek kit. I began, piece by piece, to glue together a two-foot high, intergalactic pepper pot of hatred on the table in my bedsit. This diversionary activity attracted a certain amount of derision from members of the youth club who called into my office.

'And what's so scary about a robot with a sink plunger and a whisk?' asked Den.

'Like, Tone,' commented Soup as he stared at my incomplete model, 'you're dead on and all, but sometimes I think you're a bit of a fuckin' looper.'

As winter closed in my two-bar electric heater struggled to heat the bedsit and the absence of the Super Ser made the drop-in centre truly Baltic but I kept on going in my commitment to make a difference. By the end of the year Shakin' Stevens was celebrating with 'Merry Christmas Everyone' and I was feeling more confident in my role. As 1986 dawned I secured some funding and developed a series of new projects including a senior citizens club, at which I played the guitar for a weekly sing-along of 'Daisy, Daisy' and 'The Fields of Athenry'. I started an unemployed club with adverts for jobs around the walls of the drop-in centre and arranged free driving lessons for the young people, which were intended to increase their job prospects. When I gushed of this success at one of my deputation meetings several cynics suggested we might be increasing the number of getaway drivers rather than the number of young people gaining employment. I ignored this cynicism.

The Tuesday night youth club was going from strength to

strength. It was still chaotic and unpredictable but we were making progress by introducing more educational programmes. I arranged speakers to come and talk about the dangers of alcohol and drug abuse. We developed a cross-community exchange with a Protestant youth club in Holywood and, against all expectations on both sides, no one was hurt during the visits to each others' clubs. The young people played cross-community pool and flirted across the sectarian divide as if they were normal. I even arranged for the youth club members to try yachting, which was as much a first for me as for the young people. We went out on Belfast Lough with FOCUS (Finding Out Christ Under Sail). The young people loved it while I boked into the sea for most of the trip. Then we introduced a Sunday night youth club for those who wanted to explore faith. We invited rock gospel singers, like Ken Duncan from Lisburn. Ken played techno rock gospel with a dazzling synthesiser like a Pet Shop Boy but more Christian (and less gay, of course). The Sunday night youth club was a big success with lots of good discussion about faith and social issues.

I secured a grant from the Northern Ireland Voluntary Trust Community Arts Scheme for the young people to make a film with the pensioners. Our budding Spielbergs filmed interviews with pensioners in which they asked them about their childhood memories of North Belfast. After many hours of hard work, the youth club members and I showed it to the pensioners. Our intergenerational video was such a success that the pensioners cried, the young people smiled and we even got our picture taken for the *Belfast Telegraph*. This was the first time our youth group completed a project and there was a great sense of pride in the achievement. Of course, no one got a job out of it, but the increase in self-confidence was obvious. It seemed as if I was starting to make a difference after all.

5

NO FATHER OF MINE

'That wee blade nearly had kittens when yer man told her it wouldn't be ready on time!'

I was in a queue at the passport office in Belfast behind a big woman in a floral headscarf encasing tight plastic hair curlers. She was providing me with an unsolicited running commentary on the progress of the passport application of each person in front of us.

'I'd rather have an Irish passport any day anyway!' shouted the wee blade as she departed in tears, with a definite political edge to her indignation.

'Well she'll have a helluva lot longer to wait for a Free State one,' asserted the big woman, subtly indicating to the remainder of the queue where she stood on the question of the constitutional status of Northern Ireland.

'Wee Fenian,' she whispered in my ear.

It was just another normal day in Belfast but I allowed the casual sectarianism of my fellow citizens to pass me by. I was getting married soon and I needed a passport so that I could whisk Lesley away from the peace line for an exotic – and hopefully at long last, erotic – honeymoon in the sun. I was determined to find a holiday destination beyond the radioactive fall-out zone in Europe, perhaps North Africa, where there was no danger that radiation from Chernobyl might artificially enhance our suntans. The nuclear disaster in the Soviet Union had cast a shadowy glow across the whole of Europe. There was even talk of radioactive sheep in Ballymena.

I had taken a few hours off work to submit my passport application. I felt guilty taking any time off but today I was going to be selfish and take a break for the sake of my future wife. Lesley and her mother had been planning the wedding with detailed military precision for months so the least I could do was to get my part right. I had to find and finance an exceptional honeymoon to match what was clearly intended to be the finest wedding in the history of Bellaghy.

A middle-class mid-Ulster wedding often felt light years away from our day-to-day life in the New Lodge. As I stood in the slow-moving queue I tuned out the observations of the woman in front of me by ticking off my work to do list in my head. I needed to complete an application for money to refurbish the pool table and buy new equipment for the youth club. The rips from misplayed shots and the burns from the resting cigarettes of hundreds of teenagers were bad enough, but last week when I suggested that Mo should wait his turn he had jumped on top of the pool table in his Doctor Martens, pointed the pool cue at me threateningly and called me a 'speccy bastard'. The damage to the pool table was more permanent than the injury to my feelings. We also needed a new pool cue because Tonto had used the other one as an improvised spear to fire at a passing Saracen full of British soldiers. It was like watching *Zulu* all over again. We also needed a new set of ping-pongs since Big Mickey had drawn genitalia on the current set. There was so much work to do and so little time to do it all. I was still working mornings, afternoons and evenings every day. The drop-in centre needed repainted, the broken windows needed replaced and new security grilles were urgently required following the latest break in. Then there were more funding applications, writing the prayer letter for supporters and being available to the young people in an emergency. Suddenly a tap on my shoulder and a familiar voice interrupted my thoughts.

'Hello, Mrs Piper' I said. Typically bad luck that I had bumped into my parents' most obnoxious neighbour.

'Anyway, how's your father? I hear he's been bad with his nerves since he gave up the drink.'

A silence ensued but I was determined it would be brief.

'Och, he's doing well now. He'd a wee bit of depression but he's back at work now, so he is,' I replied calmly, trying to hide my horror that this woman was apparently so well informed about my father's mental health.

'A wee spell in Purdysburn's nothing to be ashamed of, so it's not,' she said, although her disapproving eyebrows contradicted her words.

'Nixt!' shouted the imposing bespectacled gentleman behind the plastic screen at the front of the passport office, saving me from any further interaction with Mrs Piper.

'Enjoy your honeymoon, love,' said the big woman in front as she departed. 'I hope your wee girl's not one of the wrong sort.'

Once my passport papers were successfully submitted I popped around the corner to The Model Shop in Queen Street to buy a tube of glue for my ongoing model Dalek project. The last tube had mysteriously disappeared after Paddy had been to see me to ask if we would lift the ban he'd received from the youth club for spitting in a volunteer's face.

I decided to walk home up Murder Mile for some exercise because I was aware of spending far too much time sitting at a desk. On the doctor's advice I was walking more as well as playing squash with Lesley and endurance swimming against the wave machine in the Shankill Leisure Centre. As I dandered up the Antrim Road I thought about all the young people in the youth club and all the family problems they were facing – alcoholism, gambling problems, violent death, physical and mental illness. I prayed for each one and asked God to carry them through the problems in their lives. I asked God to help me to help them.

When I arrived back at the flat I hid the model glue under my wilting spider plant and got to work on the latest Children in Need application form. I was answering the question 'In what way are the children in your project disadvantaged?' with the statistic of '90 per cent youth unemployment in the New Lodge', which I was certain would shock Pudsey Bear and Terry Wogan into giving us £300 for the pool table, when the phone rang.

'Is that Tony?' asked a familiar voice. It sounded like Uncle Sammy, not my real uncle but my parents' kindly next-door neighbour, although he sounded different because his voice was shaking.

'It's Uncle Samuel. Can you come home right away?'

I could hear screaming in the background. It sounded like my mother.

'Your father's ... taken seriously ill. Can you come home right away?'

Uncle Sammy sounded as if he was distressed but was trying hard to be calm for my sake.

'He's dead!' I heard my mother screaming. 'He's dead! He's dead!'

I felt my heart thump in my chest. I could hear another woman weeping in the background. It sounded like Auntie Jean, Sammy's wife, who was a good friend to my mother.

'Can you come quickly, Tony, son?' pleaded Uncle Sammy.

I felt suddenly lightheaded and as I blinked it was as if I was out of my body and watching this scene from above.

'He's dead!' I heard my mother shriek again and again, 'He's dead! He's dead!'

'I'm coming,' I said as I slammed the phone down.

My head was spinning and as I ran into the office next door I was aware that my feet and hands were tingling. I must have looked awful because when John Evans lifted his head from the accounts, he looked at me with great concern.

'Can you give me a lift home, now please, John? My neighbour's phoned to say my father is s-s-seriously ill,' I heard myself stuttering, 'b-but I could hear m-my m-mother screaming in the b-b-background ... I think she was shouting "He's dead!"'

There was silence in the car as my mind replayed the traumatic call. My mother's grief-stricken shrieks resounded in my head.

When we arrived at the house I jumped over the familiar rickety front gate and sprinted down the driveway. I noticed the Fiat Panda was parked carefully in the garage but that the garage door was open. As I ran round the back of the house I noticed momentarily that the wooden lid of the coalbunker had been recently repaired after years of remaining broken, much to my mother's frustration. I burst through the back door and found Auntie Ella, Auntie Jean and Auntie Maureen weeping in the kitchen. The last time I had seen all my lovely childhood aunties – who were all good neighbours rather than blood relations – looking so distressed was the night our neighbour Mr Moore was shot in his car in the street and died in my mother's arms. When they looked at my face they cried even more. Auntie Ella's daughter Heather, who was a policewoman, and clearly experienced in these circumstances, ushered me into the living room. She took both of my hands and looked into my eyes.

'I'm very sorry, Tony. Your daddy has taken an overdose and he's dead,' she explained.

He IS dead, I thought.

It was true. I hadn't imagined it.

'Where's Mammy?'

I had to go to her, to hold her, to comfort her, to be a man for her.

'Upstairs with him,' said Heather with tears in her eyes.

I ran up the stairs to my parents' bedroom and when I entered the room I joined an unforgettable scene. My father was lying still on the bed in his foundry clothes, eyes closed, as if he was just sleeping. I fell to my knees beside the bed ignoring the living people around me and somehow hoping it wasn't true. But when I kissed his forehead and held his hand, his skin felt so cruelly cold. The same hand that once held mine tight whenever I was scared of the bogeyman at night now felt colder than it had ever felt in my life. As I turned away in disbelief I noticed on the bedside table a pint glass containing the dregs of a deadly cocktail of pills and milk. The same beer glass that had held far too many Carlsberg Specials in recent years was now redundant, containing nothing but the deadly residue of a much swifter poisoning. Once I had taken in this grim reality I began to become more aware of the people around me. My mother was sitting on a chair beside the bed rocking back and forward crying a deeper cry than I had ever heard. She was clutching a note in her hand. I hugged her as tightly as I could for I don't know how long.

'What am I going to do without you?' she kept asking. 'What am I going to do without you?'

She showed me the tearstained note written in my father's scrawling handwriting: 'Betty, love, you'll have a happier life without me.'

'What am I going to do without you?' my mother repeated.

I read the suicide note again.

'Betty, love, you'll have a happier life without me.'

Then I looked at my mother.

'What am I going to do without you?' she wept.

Then I looked at my dead father.

What have you done? I thought. Why have you left us? Would you rather be dead than be with us?

My mother read out the note again and again.

'How could I have a happy life without him?' she cried.

Then I felt angry. Stupid, stupid man! You were supposed to be a very clever man, you know. How many times have I heard that? How could you do this to her? How could you do this to us? How could you do this to me?

Then I felt guilty. What if I had been here? Why didn't he feel he could call me to help him? I could have stopped this. How did I miss the signs?

Auntie Ella led the minister into the room and he began to pray for us. Auntie Dot and Auntie Betty and the family doctor were here now too. As the minister prayed I turned to God in grief and pain and I felt the first of many tears flowing down my nose and cheeks and onto my chin and down my neck. The more distressed I became the more it upset everyone else so I pulled myself together and went to cry in private in my old childhood bedroom like a real man. As I lay on my bed trying to come to terms with the events of the past hour I felt angry again.

Selfish, selfish bastard, I thought.

Then I felt guilty again.

I'm angry but you were ill and you didn't know what you were doing. I was more worried about helping a shower of ungrateful wee shites on the peace line than about you being depressed. I wasn't here for you, Daddy. I'm sorry. I'm sorry, Daddy. I'm sorry. I'm sorry.

I sobbed into my childhood pillow until it was soaked.

The turmoil in my mind was interrupted when the RUC arrived. My older brother hadn't reached the house yet so I had to be interviewed as the most coherent next of kin on the scene.

The policemen were kind but it was obvious from some of the questions that they had to rule out foul play. They were just doing their job but I was offended by the suggestion that anyone in our family would want to kill my father. When the police departed I went into the sitting room for some relief from all the wailing. This was the same good room where every year my father had put up the Christmas tree and left us presents from Santa. This was the room where he introduced us to each new generation of hi-fi and speakers. I found my wee brother sitting there on his own, still in his school uniform, looking out the window in a daze. I was twenty-three years old and this was tough for an adult like me but my younger brother was sixteen years old – still at school, and he had arrived home from classes and rugby practice to find his father had killed himself.

'Are you all right?' I asked.

'What do you think?' he answered.

I hugged him.

'We'll get through this,' I said, but as his eyes searched my face, I knew that neither of us was convinced by my words at that moment.

My father's good friend Uncle Harry joined us and, putting our grief before his own, he gave us a wee talk about having to be strong young men for the sake of our mother now. By this stage, the tea-making operations were in full swing in the kitchen and wider family and friends were arriving along with sandwiches and buns and traybakes from half the street. My older brother arrived and Auntie Dot and the doctor eventually persuaded my mother to leave her husband's side and they more or less carried her down the stairs to the sitting room. She sat in the big chair of the best suite, beside the good unit with the porcelain figurines of the queens of England that my father had bought her for birthdays and Christmases and anniversaries. She just sat there with a box of tissues, staring, weeping and biting her nails furiously. The ambulance arrived, a little late, I thought. I had never before encountered so many emergency services in such a sort space of time. My father's body was removed from the house. We watched through the windows of the sitting room as the stretcher transferred his remains into the redundant vehicle.

'I never thought I'd see him leave this house like this,' cried my mother in wide-eyed disbelief. I felt sick.

As the ambulance drove off Lesley arrived and I went to her immediately. She didn't need to say anything and she just held me for a while. I needed to get out of the house, so after a while we slipped away and Lesley took me to Cavehill Country Park, which overlooks the city. We walked along the side of the Cavehill in the rain. I repeated the events of the day, the phone call at work, the beer glass with the deadly potion, my mother's screams and the suicide note. Lesley listened as I repeated the details again and again until I truly believed it all. She held my hand and we walked and talked and embraced. The strange mix of conflicting emotions confused me. I was shocked and sad and angry and guilty all at the same time.

'He always said "no son of his" should do this or do that. "No son of mine is going to look down his nose at no one." "No son of mine is going to spend his life working for buttons in no dirty foundry." Well, no father of mine should ever have done what he did today. No father of mine should kill himself and break his wife's heart seven months before his son's wedding day. Did he not want to come to our wedding? He's certainly wrecked it now.'

Lesley said it was okay to be angry and I explained how guilty I felt.

'I'm so busy out to save the whole bloody world and I couldn't even save my own father,' I cried.

Lesley listened and didn't judge me and just loved me the way she always did. As we sat together in silence on a park bench overlooking Belfast Lough I gradually felt an unexpected peace overwhelm me. Maybe it was Lesley's love, maybe it was my father's spirit, perhaps it was God carrying me through the storm. Maybe I was in shock or just more resilient than I thought. When I returned to the house I acted as the strong person people expected me to be.

I awoke the next day and it dawned on me that it had not been a bad dream. I prayed for strength for the awful day ahead. When I got up I could feel the pain of loss as a gnawing ache in my limbs. It hurt to clench the fingers on my hands. However as the day went on I noticed that although I felt more bereft, shaken and upset than I had ever been in my life, I was not completely devastated. I was still me. I was broken-hearted but I was not broken. Of course I immediately felt guilty again for not being completely torn apart emotionally. But I had a choice to make and I decided that day I was not going to be a victim of this. No son of his was going to be no victim of no one! I had an unexpected assurance that I was strong enough to get through this loss and pain. I had an early sense that with the help of God and family and friends I would survive this. I don't know where this strength came from but in the days ahead it settled at my core. I made a conscious choice that I would survive this awful hurt in my life.

On the day of the funeral, we three Macaulay boys walked behind the coffin of our father Eric. Hundreds of people gathered at Wilton's Funeral Home on the Crumlin Road. Men from Mackie's foundry, neighbours from our estate and couples who had met at the Westy Disco my parents had helped to run. Even some local politicians were there to pay their respects, along with the same family and friends who would shortly be receiving wedding invitations for my happy day. I stood shoulder-to-shoulder with my brothers to welcome people to the funeral chapel, which was too small to contain all of the mourners. I shook hundreds of hands. Everyone asked how my poor mother was doing. Everybody said they were very sorry for my loss, so they were, and all of them agreed that my father had been a great fella, so he had.

'I'll never forget what your Mammy and Daddy did for us at that wee disco every Saturday night.'

'He was a very well-respected man in that foundry, son. He was fair to all the men, no matter what.'

'He was a decent crater, so he was. We're all praying for youse in the church.'

'He loved you three wee boys. You were his whole life.'

Clearly not, I thought, bitterly.

'Is the wedding still on?' asked several sincere mourners.

'Of course it is. It's what he would have wanted.' I replied, while at the same time wondering afresh why my own father had gone to such extremes to avoid giving a speech on my big day.

'Don't worry, I won't tell anyone how he died,' whispered Mrs Piper.

'He took his own life,' I replied. 'It's not a secret.'

'It's nothing to be ashamed of,' she said.

'I'm not ashamed.' I replied curtly. 'Depression is an illness like any other. There's no shame in being ill.'

All the men did their respective lifts of the coffin and as we followed the hearse down the Crumlin Road I could see the sombre young faces of me and my brothers reflected in the smoked glass of the rear window of the hearse. We looked so sad but united and strong at the same time. Then we boarded the funeral cars, similar to the wedding cars we would soon use, and we followed the hearse to Roselawn Crematorium where most of the dearly departed of Belfast were turned to ashes. As the coffin descended into the fire I held my mother's hand. This was the worst part. It felt as if the flesh of my mother's heart was tearing apart right beside me and I knew she would never heal. I sat there on the hard, cold wooden pew in sullen grief until I once again had to lead the shaking of the hands of a multitude of mourners who genuinely didn't know what to say. I didn't know what to say either. By the end of the day I was exhausted with the polite public condolences and my mix of conflicting emotions. The only thing I knew for certain was that these last three days had changed my life forever.

A few weeks later on the far side of Roselawn Cemetery we planted a tree in my father's memory. We placed a small plaque at the foot of the trunk engraved with the words:

On the first day I visited the ash tree I suddenly remembered a conversation I had had with my father shortly before he died. He had been giving me a lift when, out of the blue, he'd said, 'When my father died, I thought I would never get over it, son. I was heartbroken. I thought it was the end of the world. But I was all right in the end.'

I now understood what he was trying to say to me. It hurt so much I could still feel the loss as a physical sensation. My chest ached and my arms hurt as if I had been stretched on a rack. I had a deep and constant pain in the palms of my hands. But I knew in my heart, just as he had said, that I would be all right in the end.

A few months later I borrowed the Fiat Panda to visit my father's tree. It was a typical wet and windy day in the hills east of Belfast and the ash sapling bent a little in the wind. I spoke to my father and thanked him for all the sacrifices he had made for me and for giving me a happy childhood and a good start in life. I must have looked odd standing there with rain and tears on my cheeks, talking to a little tree. I told him I forgave him for leaving us and said I was sorry I hadn't been there to stop him killing himself. I told him he had been a good father.

When I got back into the shelter of the car to drive back to my mother's house I heard the warm voice of Candy Devine on

Downtown Radio introducing a classic hit from the 1960s by Engelbert Humperdinck. From the first few notes I recognised my parents' favourite song, 'The Last Waltz'. This was the song they had danced to the night they won the ballroom dancing competition at Butlin's in Mosney in 1977. I remembered my fourteen-year-old self watching with pride as my mother and father glided together to victory across the faded glory of the Butlin's ballroom. Then I remembered that this song was always the final 45 my father played when he was the DJ at the Westy Disco on Saturday nights in the 1970s. The young people of the Upper Shankill understood that 'The Last Waltz' meant the disco was over for another week and the dance floor cleared as throngs of teenagers made their way out of the Nissen hut for a chippy or a snog or both. But I knew the song had a deeper meaning. Every Saturday night my father was reminding my mother that he loved her. I turned up the radio so that 'The Last Waltz' would drown out my sobs.

'I had the last waltz with you,
Two lonely people together,
I fell in love with you,
The last waltz should last forever ...'

6

SUMMER NIGHTS

'Orange bastards,' shouted Mo in the direction of the approaching Orange Order parade.

'Unionist triumphalism,' sneered Gerry.

'Five hundred years of British oppression!' shouted Den.

I was standing with a group of youth club members and a few of my neighbours in front of a line of fifty-foot-high steel barriers that cut across the main Antrim Road. The British army had carried out this impressive feat of engineering earlier that morning, forming a temporary peace wall to block the road and stop us from killing each other. The ingenuity and money available to keep us apart knew no bounds. Dozens of police Land Rovers and army tanks held the barriers in place while scores of soldiers and armed policemen stood with their backs to us, facing the parade. This choice of stance suggested whose side they were on. Through gaps in the barriers we caught glimpses of rows of older men in bowler hats with orange sashes marching and carrying their banners, followed by younger men in baseball caps with blue plastic bags marching and carrying their beer cans.

'Sorry about your da, Tone,' said Billy quietly, arriving late to the scene before turning his attention to the British army and starting to roar, 'Brits Out! Brits Out!'

'Fuckin' huns!' shouted Tonto at the top of his voice, jumping up and down as if he might just see over the top of the barriers.

'Fenian bastards!' replied a snarling Orangeman. I could see through the fence that he was almost dribbling onto his collarette.

It was a normal summer Saturday in North Belfast. Today was the day of a big parade and the security forces had blocked the road so that the Orangemen could follow their traditional route through a neighbourhood where few Protestants lived any more. The young people had got up much earlier than usual just to be offended by this outrage. I had got up at my usual time and I was quite outraged myself. The security barriers had blocked me in. I was annoyed because I had been unable to get to the shop to buy milk for my cornflakes. In fact I couldn't really go anywhere until the march was over. If the marchers didn't hurry up I was going to be late for a date with Lesley to see *Police Academy 3*.

'Ya see, ya see!' cried Den, pointing at the passing Orange parade, 'You wouldn't believe what it was like! We get blocked in all the time, like second-class citizens so they can march through our areas!'

I refused to accept the whole idea of 'our area' and 'their area' and generally went wherever I wanted in Belfast. Today in the city you still hear people talking about an area being Protestant or Catholic, republican or loyalist, as if a group of streets and buildings could have a political identity, or about Catholic and Protestant houses, as if buildings, like their residents, were also aligned with a church they didn't go to. The land beneath these streets was here long before these manmade identities claimed it and I'm sure our land will remain when the current residents and our selfish squabbles are buried beneath it.

'I know, I see,' I replied. Where I had grown up an Orange Order parade was a family event at which children in prams waved mini flags at their grandas and mothers handed out egg and onion sandwiches and cups of tea in plastic tumblers. Today I was experiencing an Orange parade in different moccasins. I felt hemmed in and I didn't like it.

The young people seemed to hate Orangemen even more than they hated the Brits, which was very worrying because even if the IRA did manage to bomb the Brits out, they would have a much bigger job on their hands forcing out the hundreds of thousands of Orangemen who lived all over Northern Ireland.

'Come on lads, stop the sectarian name calling,' I said, aware I was sounding a tad sanctimonious in the circumstances. I knew it wouldn't take much for this situation to descend into violence. The young people would justify their part in any street disturbances from their sense of injustice and I feared they would end up being hurt or arrested. This was a practical opportunity for me to try to prevent that.

'They're the bigots,' interrupted Mo. 'The Brits and the peelers have blocked us in so themuns can march and wave their flegs at us over batin' the Catholics in some battle in 16-fuckin'-90.'

'I know, but lads, do you not think you're being a wee bit sectarian yourselves, comin' down here just to shout abuse at them?' I dared to ask.

My gentle challenge was undermined by the arrival of several empty beer cans and a red brick over the top of the barrier, accompanied by a heightened volume of drumming, along with shouts of 'Yeeooooow!' and 'Kill all taigs!'

'Ya see, ya see, Tony. That's how sectarian they are! Sectarian Prod bastards – every fuckin' one of them,' said Den.

'But lads, are you not makin' yourselves just as bad as them by shoutin' back?' I ventured.

'They're the bigots and guess what? Cilla Black! Surprise, sur-fuckin'-prise! The Brits and the RUC are helpin' them,' said Gerry.

'We don't want no Orange feet on our roads!' said Mo.

'Kill All Prods!' shouted Billy.

It was clear that the conversation was over. An assault on the dividing fences and the RUC was brewing. My influence was proving to be limited and if I wasn't careful I could find myself in a crowd attacking the police.

I returned to the bedsit for a depressing bowl of dry cornflakes as a riot developed outside my window.

Summers in Belfast were for fighting. It wasn't a proper summer on the peace lines without riots – for us youth workers in North Belfast, they were part of the annual calendar. The advent of petrol bombs at the peace line in the marching season was just as predictable as the arrival of the Baby Jesus at Christmas. This was turning out to be a good year for riots because of the Anglo-Irish Agreement, which was signed in November 1985. Unionists were so outraged by the agreement, which gave the Irish government an advisory role in the government of Northern Ireland, that young working-class Protestants now had tacit permission to attack the police with as much vigour as the other side. Meanwhile, republicans saw riots as the best way to show that our sectarian statelet had failed, so they were well worth the sacrifice of their disaffected youth. While the politicians spoke out from the comfort of television studios, the poorest young men in their communities were on the streets, injured or imprisoned or both for acting out the anger of their leaders and their communities. I had always mistrusted politicians and their sectarian sound bites about how much we needed to vote for them to keep the other side out. To be fair, the fact they never did much more for the people than keep the other side out was at least sticking to their manifestos. Ultimately this was the only thing that most people cared about so they voted the same men back in every time and the areas of highest social deprivation and worst educational achievement never improved. The young men who answered the call and did all the rioting remained poor and forgotten. Going to live on the other side contradicted everything most politicians in Belfast stood for. Perhaps my decision was political in the sense that it was anti-political – anti- every sectarian political diatribe. I was learning more and more every day by living on the other side. In fact I was beginning to think it should be made compulsory and then we would all wise up, understand each other better and catch ourselves on.

Orange parades and bonfires were an important part of the culture I was born into but they weren't important to me. In my youth I had enjoyed the boneys on the Eleventh Night – groups of friends building and guarding a bonfire and then a party around it, baking potatoes in tinfoil. This was long before the bonfires became the property of local paramilitary gangsters, who turned them into industrial mega-boneys and built them with with lorry loads of tyres and wooden pallets, all in the name of displaying control of 'their' communities. I regretted that bonfire nights were increasingly dominated by underage drinking, paramilitary displays and burning Irish flags.

I always found the endless marching to the same old musical repertoire on the Twelfth incredibly boring. Some families were devoted to the Orange Order and the bands tradition and gave hours to their cultural heritage but my family had largely become distanced from all of that, though they still went to watch the marches on the Twelfth itself. Both my grandfathers had been Orangemen and my father marched on the Twelfth in his youth, but when the Troubles started he felt the Orange Order was too closely associated with paramilitaries. In fact I was forbidden by him from joining the Orange Order. This was ironic, as I was never invited to join. It's even more ironic that the Orange Order is the only organisation that has never asked me to join that has members who have expressed resentment towards me for not being a member. It's a bit like not being invited to a family wedding and then being criticised for not going by the people who never invited you. Of course I had no intention of joining the Orange Order. Apart from the obvious clash with my belief that Christians were called to make peace rather than celebrate a battle victory, from an early age had I connected Orange parades and Orange halls with alcohol abuse. My immersion in evangelical religious tradition combined with revulsion at my father's heavy drinking meant that I was teetotal. As a teenager I taught Sunday School every week in an Orange hall. My abiding memory is not of banners expressing loyalty to God or the Queen but the smell of stale beer that had been spilled on the tables the night before. Although there were thousands of flags waved every Twelfth they were far outnumbered by the tens of thousands of units of alcohol consumed. None of the religious organisations I was involved in permitted alcohol at any of their events, not even a glass of wine at the Sunday School teachers' Christmas dinner. I often wondered how sincere these marching men were about God. They clearly loved their country and had great pride in their cultural heritage, but it seemed to me that for most of them, the religious part was more about cultural Protestantism than faith in God. There were Orange services in the church all the time but very few of the men who came to these services ever came to church otherwise, unless it was with a flag and a band, a baby, a bride or in a coffin. When I saw Orange leaders speak on TV some of them sounded sincerely religious and I wondered why they had allowed their organisation to become so publicly irreligious with drunk and disorderly events. Either they weren't as sincere as they appeared or perhaps my father had been right, and they were afraid to stand up to the paramilitaries who loved their beer almost as much as they loved Ulster. My father, my late father, was a very clever man, you know.

Although summer in Belfast was all about our culture or their culture or two competing cultures I noticed we had a shared culture. Living on the other side revealed to me that we shared a deeply embedded culture of blame, violence and sectarianism.

To distract the youth of the New Lodge, we organised summer

schemes and trips away from the city as an alternative to rioting. We advertised the summer scheme by walking along the streets and parks on summer nights, chatting to young people and giving out leaflets inviting them to sign up. I generally got a warm response – albeit with an appropriate degree of slegging about being a snobby Christian and a speccy bastard. I felt safe most of the time, even though it was obvious I was a Protestant from the Saltshaker Centre walking around a republican area. Some people told me my head was away and that taking this risk was suicidal, but I felt safe and I had recently learned from bitter experience about people who were truly suicidal. The truth is that beneath the nasty sectarian exterior many Belfast people are much more tolerant than you would expect, especially face to face.

One of the best places for advertising the summer scheme was at the Waterworks, one of the largest parks in North Belfast. In the nineteenth century the Belfast Waterworks had been reservoirs, supplying water to the city's factories and residents. When demand began to outstrip supply and new reservoirs were created, the area was transformed into a leisure park, complete with boating and outdoor swimming. During the Second World War, the German bombers mistook the Waterworks for the shipyard and many lives were lost in the surrounding streets. But by the 1980s the days of genteel rowing boats, public bathing and swimming galas were a distant memory. This once-beautiful park was now the scene of an ugly sectarian turf war. For many people it was important to establish whether the ripples covering submerged shopping trolleys from Stewart's Supermarket were British or Irish waters. The top end of the Waterworks (beside the Westland Road) was Protestant and the bottom part of the Waterworks (beside the Antrim Road) was Catholic. Unionists walked their Protestant dogs in the top end of the park, while republican young people drank their Catholic cider in the bottom end. On summer nights we walked through the parks in pairs and had many good conversations with bored teenagers about how fed up they were with Belfast and how it was all other side's fault. I always knew it was time to withdraw when the drink-fuelled talk became more aggressive or when some of the gangs' attention was drawn to the presence of the enemy in the form of the other side, the police, the army or 'yer man that moans to our mas about us drinkin' in the park'. However, we managed to attract some of the bored youth from the bottom end of the Waterworks to our summer scheme trips. Obviously our trips weren't as exciting as petrol bombing a Protestant pensioner's house for equal rights, but some of them were very eventful. Our barbecues were remarkably trouble free, which proved to me that there was nothing wrong with our young people; it was the social and political environment that brought out the worst in them. Many had never been to the places we visited before even though most of our destinations were less than an hour from Belfast. Our barbecues to Drain's Bay on the Antrim Coast Road were a mixture of hide and seek, games, races, hunts, hot dogs with tomato ketchup and bottles of Orangeade. Things did get a bit more exciting on one occasion when Ciaran announced he would be waiting in the bushes beside the car park if anyone wanted to join him for sex. No one dared to enter the bushes to retrieve him, but fortunately only one girl had to be pulled out of his thorny den by the feet before she got too close. Our trips to Tollymore Forest Park required strict adherence to minibus etiquette to ensure our vehicle wasn't stoned, hijacked or burned. No sectarian songs were permitted during the journey, although Gerry argued that a rebel song was not a sectarian song and we finally allowed 'The Fields of Athenry'. Giving the finger to pedestrians in streets with red, white and blue painted kerbstones and cheering triumphantly when we entered a town or village with Irish Tricolors on the lampposts were usually the highlights of the journey. It was like being in a travelling pantomime where you booed the bad streets and cheered the good. This reminded me of my many trips away with the Westy Disco when I was a teenager, except that the boos and cheers were in reverse. A team of summer scheme volunteers joined us and slept on the floor of the church hall for two weeks. These students from Northern Ireland, England and the USA supported the regular youth club leaders who knew the young people better, and had vital knowledge like who was most likely to smuggle drink on to the minibus or start a fight on the way home. It was clear that getting away from the tensions and experiencing even slightly wider horizons was a positive experience for most of the young people whose world was often defined about where to go and not to go to avoid getting your head kicked in.

One of our most popular summer scheme trips was the children's trip to Belfast Zoo at the top of the Antrim Road. It was inexpensive, we could reach it quickly, without crossing any peace lines, and the children loved the animals. It was the annual highlight for the younger kids on the summer scheme. This year, as leader-in-charge of the trip, I was excited about making sure everyone had a happy day out. The day was already hot when we arrived there in two minibuses with thirty primary-school-age children and thirty plastic bags containing packed lunches of cheese sandwiches the volunteers had prepared the night before along with crisps and cheap pop. All went well until we arrived at the prairie dogs' enclosure. Dozens of these mischievous little rodents lived in large underground burrows beneath mounds of dirt where they sat alert and scanning for predators. Such was their enthusiasm for breeding, the prairie dogs seemed to be taking over a whole section of the zoo almost the whole way down to the derelict 1930s art deco ballroom, the Floral Hall, a sad relic of the age of Belfast show bands and dances. The drama began when the ginger twins who were on the trip climbed over the low wall into the enclosure.

'Boys, get outta there now before they bite you!' I shouted after them.

The zookeeper arrived on the scene promptly.

'Can you not control them wee hallions?' he asked.

The other twenty-eight children were squealing with delight at the sight of the twins chasing scores of the little creatures in every direction.

'Twins, will youse two get outta there now!' I shouted, but the laughing boys were oblivious to anything outside of the enclosure.

How will I tell their mother that I let her twins get rabies? I wondered.

'Boys if you don't get outta there now you're banned from the next trip to Drain's Bay!' I threatened.

The other children were now squealing with excitement.

'Can you not control them?!' said the zookeeper, red-faced and angry.

Er, not really, I thought.

'Of course I can!' I replied indignantly.

'They are in great danger,' shouted the zookeeper.

'I'm the youth leader in charge,' I explained as calmly as possible. 'I'm sorry they won't come out. They'll get bored soon.'

'They are in great danger,' he repeated into his walkie-talkie.

Now I was starting to panic. I was going to be responsible for the twins being mauled to death by a pack of prairie dogs. Then I spotted, with some relief, a notice saying that the prairie dogs were herbivores.

'How much danger are the children in?' I asked urgently.

'I'm not talkin' about the wee lads, son,' replied the zookeeper. 'I was talkin' about the bloody prairie dogs.'

Yes, it was a typical summer in Belfast, and while the fighting continued in the streets below, on a hot summer day in 1986 in a beautiful zoo on the slopes of the Cavehill the ginger twins and the prairie dogs had the best time ever.

Later when I tried to tell Lesley this story I could barely get through it without laughing. I laughed until I cried. It felt good to cry not out of grief.

7

THE LITTLE HOUSE

Our wedding was just five months away and we still hadn't found anywhere to live. The bedsit was all right for me, but Lesley was used to more comfortable accommodation. One fateful day I was driving down Clifton Park Avenue, which was just around the corner from 174 Antrim Road. I was on my way to visit my mother, to see how she was and to find out if the bereavement counselling was helping, when I noticed building work right beside the peace line, on a small patch of wasteland next to the crumbling premises of the Cat Protection League. A small row of houses was being built under the shadow of the massive wall that surrounded Girdwood army barracks and stretched the whole way to the rear of Crumlin Road Prison. This steel-clad, barbed-wire-topped monstrosity acted both as a perimeter fence for the British army base and a peace wall between the Protestants at the Crumlin Road end of Clifton Park Avenue and the Catholics here at the Antrim Road end. Clifton Park Avenue had once been one of the finest streets in Belfast, with beautiful three- and four-storey terraced houses inhabited by lawyers who worked in the nearby Crumlin Road courthouse, doctors from the nearby

Mater Hospital and well-heeled business owners and managers. Today this former tree-lined avenue was mostly waste ground. The middle classes had moved out in droves at the start of the Troubles and, one by one, their abandoned houses were burnt to the ground, demolished or converted into squalid flats. The gaps left behind by the rows of huge town houses that had been reduced to rubble created a sort of 'no man's land' between the two sections of the community, which suited everybody. When it rained, as if often did, the street looked like a post-apocalyptic scene from a science fiction movie.

As well as being in the shadow of the barracks, the building work was also beside a sizeable house that was the premises of the Belfast Cat Protection League, known locally as the cats' home. Once one of the most prestigious detached Victorian residences of Clifton Park Avenue, it was now really only safe for stray cats. The cats were neither Protestant nor Catholic, so were safer than most residents living on the peace line. Just across the road from the building site and nearest to the Protestant side of the peace line was a solitary terraced house. It looked very odd just sitting there all alone. This terraced property had once been only one sliver of a residence in a street full of dozens of terraced houses in a long-since demolished community. The house reminded me of a single playing card that was somehow defying the laws of physics and still standing after the rest of the house of cards had been removed. On the external walls of the upper floor you could still see old-fashioned patterned wallpaper from the bedrooms of the houses that had once been attached on either side. The elderly resident of this last house standing had refused to move from his home while everything around him had been demolished. In front of the house was nothing but waste ground scattered with dumped furniture, rusting car parts, cement blocks, broken glass and crumbling red bricks.

A few weeks later I was driving past the building site again en route to the Shankill Leisure Centre for a game of squash and a 20p session on a sunbed. This time I noticed a large sign advertising houses for sale in the small development, which had been named Brucevale Park. The billboard was so attractive that you would have thought the houses were being built somewhere normal. When I saw this sign my first thought was 'Who in their right mind would want to buy a house there?' The development was so close to the peace line that it would automatically be a target for sectarian attacks by drunken loyalists on the Eleventh night and probably any other night of the year, with or without the motivator of cultural celebrations or Buckfast. The little houses would automatically become the first line of defence for the nationalist community along this section of the peace line. In addition, they were located right beside an army base, which could be targeted with an IRA gun or mortar bomb attack at any moment. Sometimes the mortar bombs missed and the neighbouring buildings and their residents were the collateral damage. The IRA sometimes described such death and destruction as 'regrettable', which was the sort of word I would have used to describe the cancellation of an episode of *Doctor Who* rather than the murder of a human being.

But for the next few weeks, every time I passed the building site I was drawn to have a closer look. The small red-brown brick homes were advertised as 'town houses' but had little in common with the grand old town houses that once lined Clifton Park Avenue. However they looked fresh and attractive, particularly in contrast to all the old blocked up houses in the surrounding streets. Priced at £18,500 these 'luxury homes' were available on the co-ownership scheme for people on low incomes. This allowed you to buy half the house with a mortgage from a building society; the scheme bought the other half and then rented it back to you.

With each week that passed, I found myself thinking about these new houses more and more. They were in the right location for my work, at the right price for first-time buyers, and much more attractive and habitable than most of the private rental sector properties I had seen.

Who would want to live there? I asked myself.

Me, I finally concluded.

Us? I wondered, thinking of my wife to be.

Yes, the INLA graffiti on the wall beside the building site was off-putting. We certainly needed to weigh up the risk of attacks from loyalists and republicans. But the more I thought and prayed about it, the more I became convinced that this would be the perfect place for us to start our married life. I decided to broach the subject with Lesley.

'I found us a brand new house in the perfect location,' I told Lesley excitedly.

My fiancée gave me one of her 'Uh oh, what's he come up with this time?' looks.

'Well, it's on the peace line but it's the perfect location for us,' I ventured.

'Is it nice?' asked Lesley.

'I think so.'

'Is it safe?'

'I think so.'

'Can we afford it?'

'I think so.'

The next day we visited the estate agent and picked up a colour brochure with the plans for the development and the layout of the individual houses. The houses were very small but big enough for just the two of us. I took Lesley round to the building site to explain how ideal it was and how safe it would be. Lesley didn't say much, which was highly unusual, so at first I was worried that she might hate the idea and we would be back to the drawing board. This was not exactly the sort of place that Lesley had ever imagined living. I knew she wouldn't be put off by the INLA graffiti because Lesley had grown up as one of the minority of Protestants in the South Derry village of Bellaghy where the INLA was particularly popular and her next-door neighbour had been their most famous leader, Dominic McGlinchey. Lesley and I both believed that you sometimes had to take radical steps for peace, but this was going quite far. How many fiancées in their right mind would want to set up house on Murder Mile? None of the other staff or volunteers of the 174 Trust had ever done anything like this before. Renting in the inner city was unusual enough for people who didn't come from round here, but putting your life savings into a house on the peace line was taking a big gamble. Even Rev. Taylor himself didn't own the besieged manse he lived in and he could simply move out when the time came for him to minister in a different church.

'Well I know it's probably only for a few years, but if we ever want to move house no one will want to buy it from us,' said Lesley.

However Lesley's main concerns were more about the proximity to the army barracks, the possibility of projectiles being thrown over the peace wall and the surrounding grim urban dereliction. She had lived in a small rural village for most of her life. The only thing this place had in common with rural South Derry was enthusiasm for the INLA. The artist's drawing on the property sale brochure suggested that the new development would look quite attractive with private parking spaces and a green area with a few trees. The artist's landscape did not include a representation of the desolation just across the road. Clifton Park Avenue looked like a 1940s street in London after the Blitz. I believed there was a possibility that Brucevale Park could become a little oasis on the peace line, and I explained to Lesley that if we bought one of the houses in the back row in the middle, it would be safer. The houses at the end of the row were at risk of being attacked by drunken Protestants who ventured across no man's land with a brick or two. In fact the windows of the two brand new end-terrace houses had been smashed already. The windows were boarded up before the houses were even sold! On the other hand, if any angry nationalists ever decided to burn us out for being Protestants living in 'their' community, I figured it was better to live in the middle of the row, where we would be harder to find and from where it would be easier to escape to safety across the peace line to the Protestant side. I had it all worked out. I also thought that the back row was more private and would make our house less of a sitting duck for any passing drunken youth club members who had been barred for sniffing glue in the toilets, even if it was facing the army base. I reassured Lesley that at least the back garden of the cats' home was between our house and the security wall, and – if I were a member of the IRA – I would probably mortar bomb the army barracks from a more strategic position than this anyway.

Lesley wisely suggested we waited until we could have a look inside the house and see how safe it felt before making a decision. In the meantime I showed the building site to various friends and family members and the responses ranged from 'Are you sure about this?' to 'You're not near right in the head, wee lad!' My mother had other things on her mind and did not object too strongly to our proposed peace line home although she voiced some concerns about our safety. 'You'd better look after that wee girl if you're gonna live over there' was her advice.

Lesley's parents travelled down to Belfast to view the house and seemed somewhat cautious but not strongly opposed to the idea.

'I'm surprised they're dead on about you living here,' I said. 'I thought they'd be horrified, not knowing Belfast and all.'

'They've no idea!' replied Lesley. 'It's all just Belfast to them.'

Of course, Lesley's parents were well aware that once their only child had decided on what she wanted to do, any efforts to dissuade her would be pointless.

I was determined, committed and zealous and no one was going to put me off. I was convinced that once Lesley and I bought a house on the peace line lots of other committed Christian activists would follow and that this peace movement would ultimately transform the whole area – from segregation to integration and from fear to peace. I was almost certain I was completely right about this, but sometimes from his grave I could hear my father whispering in my ear, 'Your head's in cloud bloody cuckoo land, son.'

Eventually we went for a viewing. As we waited outside in the street I noticed that from here you could see the top of the imposing granite tower of the Crombie Building at Belfast Royal Academy, which was just around the corner on the Cliftonville Road. It struck me that although I was living and working within a few yards of my old school, my life and experiences now felt a million miles away from the protected cocoon of the prestigious grammar school. A few weeks ago I had contacted the school to warn the headmaster about an incident at the bus stop outside the Saltshaker Centre. I had had to distract an angry lad just out of prison who was about to beat up a naive fourth former from BRA who had not taken the school's advice to avoid the bus stops at the top of the New Lodge Road. The schools in North Belfast had an agreement to co-ordinate the school day so that Protestants and Catholics were less likely to meet each other after school on the streets. In addition, pupils at BRA were advised that the bus stops above the Cliftonville Road were for them while the bus stops below this junction were for students from St Malachy's. This was all part of our grammar school education and, to be fair, most of the clever children could have passed an eleven-plus in avoiding the other side. Just as the bespectacled scholar was about to get his head kicked in for being a 'snobby Orange bastard' I intervened with a friendly chat about how welcome the aggressor would be to join the unemployed club at the Saltshaker Centre.

'Wha?' he said.

'It's dead on, we can help you with job applications and getting ready for interviews and everything,' I explained, as the bus arrived and the swot boarded to be transported to the safety of Ben Madigan.

It didn't take very long to view the house because it was so small. I was relieved that it had a normal doorbell rather then the grating buzzer that had been shredding my nerves for months now at the bedsit. The downstairs was one large room with a bay window looking into the crumbling old red brick perimeter wall of the cats' home. There was space for a fireplace, and for a small kitchen that we could choose. Upstairs there was a tiny plastic bathroom and two bedrooms overlooking the army barracks – although as the barbed wire top of the fencing and the security spotlights were higher than the roof of the house I suppose the barracks overlooked us. It was hard to tell if anyone was really looking into the bedrooms from the military lookout posts. The bedrooms also had views of the back garden of the cats' home, where dozens of cats were climbing trees, meowing and licking their paws in the shadow of the 50-foot security wall.

Outside the house there was a side gate made of black painted wooden panels, a tiny garden, a space for the bin and a coalbunker for the open fire that heated the house. It was a modest little house but it was brand new and surprisingly bright given that it was so thoroughly overshadowed and surrounded by the architecture of war. I watched Lesley's face as the estate agent showed us around and did his best to explain that this was a safe and improving location where house prices were rising and where there was really very little trouble at all.

Aye, dead on! I thought.

When the estate agent departed we stood outside, breathed in the damp air, soaked up the environment and looked around us for a long time. Lesley was uncharacteristically silent. Growing up in a big house in a country village, she wasn't used to having so many neighbours in such close proximity. This community was much closer to my working-class roots. I blended in here in my denims but Lesley was immaculately dressed as usual and looked rather out of place.

'Well?' I asked Lesley.

She looked around again and again, casting her eyes from the dereliction across the road to the INLA graffiti on the wall behind us to the security wall of the army barracks in front of us and back to the modest little house itself.

'Well, I could make that wee house lovely,' she said with a smile.

I knew Lesley could make anywhere lovely just by being there. I was so lucky to be sharing my life with someone who shared my dreams and convictions and who was even prepared to consider taking this massive step for God, for peace and for me.

'Will we go for it?' I asked.

Lesley thought for another while.

Finally she turned to me and took a deep breath.

'Oh my nerves, wee lad, you've no idea,' she said, more quietly and calmly than usual.

We had decided to buy our little house on the peace line.

8

CHILDREN IN NEED

'Who was it?' I asked through clenched teeth. I was trying not to vent the full force of my exasperation.

The entire youth club shrugged simultaneously.

'Who flushed the friggin' Connect 4 tokens down the bog?'

Several sniggers but no reply.

'If no one's man enough to own up,' I said, eyeing Den, 'then you'll all be barred. Every single one of youse.'

Heads down. Multiple cigarette drags. Silence.

I was making a threat I knew I would not carry out, like a Secretary of State for Northern Ireland. I explained that now we'd need to buy a new set and get a plumber to unblock the train. Expense we could do without after having had to buy a new Super Ser to replace the one Mick had nicked.

'Why would anyone want to ruin their own youth club anyway?' I asked.

'Cause it's borin' as fuck,' said Gerry.

'Pure shite,' contributed Tonto.

Their opinions weren't news to me but they were still soul destroying.

'It's your club, so it is. So what do you want to do?'

The suggestions included more girls at the club, more trips, more scuffles … after which a minor scuffle developed.

'Doesn't yer man Terry Wogan give yousens money sometimes?' asked Tonto.

'Yes, we got a grant last year,' I said.

'So why don't we raise money for Children In Need?' asked Jeff.

'Sure we're not children in need,' said Soup.

'Aye,' said Jeff, 'but we should do it to help all them poor wee kids with nathin'.'

This comment was followed by only two 'wise a baps' and one 'catch yerself on' indicating that the suggestion might have some potential.

'Houl yer horses, lads!' I said, 'I think that's a great idea! So, how would you raise money for Children in Need? A sponsored walk?'

'Sponsored walk, my arse!' said Gerry, 'You're not at Belfast Royal Academy now, so you're nat. All you Prods ever wanna do is walk or fuckin' march!'

'A sponsored piss up!' suggested Billy.

'Sponsored scuffles!' cheered the lads.

Once the latest scuffle calmed down, Soup came up with a more practical suggestion.

'What about a five-a-side football tournament?' said Soup.

'What about a sponsored pool competition?' asked Jeff.

This seemed like a pretty good idea to me.

'Aye, we could do it in here,' said Gerry, as he hackled into his ashtray.

The young people were so brutalised by the Troubles that the last time they had been this excited was when a British soldier was shot. I thought the five-a-side football team was the better idea, but my youth work training had taught me to take the lead from the young people. Of course, this particular youth work methodology didn't work so well when all the young people wanted to do was to break a few Orange bastards' windows in Tiger's Bay.

Within a few minutes, and after a sustained period of intriguing whispering, nodding and winking among several youth club members, everyone agreed on a twenty-four-hour pool tournament, with all the players being sponsored by the hour.

'When will we do it? The marra?' asked Den.

'No, lads, we need time to plan it properly and get permission and everything,' I explained, trying not to dampen this new-found enthusiasm.

One of the biggest problems of long-term unemployment and the severe lack of job opportunities for our young people was the feeling of hopelessness that resulted in apathy. At least bombs and shootings and riots were exciting. Enthusiasm was rare because the young people found it hard to dream of a better life, and attempts to break out of the pattern of unemployment and poverty had proved fruitless. For example, I had recently arranged a job interview for Soup in a hardware shop in the city centre. He would have been a good employee but he clammed up at the interview and the shopkeeper didn't want to take a risk with a young lad from the New Lodge. Soup's conclusion was that he would never get a job.

The enthusiasm for the fundraiser remained and the stage was set. The first Saltshaker Senior Youth Club Sponsored Twenty-four-hour Pool Tournament would take place in November, on the night of the BBC Children in Need telethon. Everyone got busy making the necessary arrangements. I had to seek permission from John Evans and give Rev. Taylor assurances we would have adequate volunteers to supervise the twenty-four hours and that the young people wouldn't be allowed to wreck the place, bring in alcohol or run off with the sponsorship money. I was more than 50 per cent certain I could avert all of these possibilities. Next we had to design and print the sponsorship forms and give them out to the youth club members and then arrange a rota for both youth workers and pool players to cover half-hour sessions for a period of twenty-four hours. I was delighted when some of the young people got busy asking family and neighbours for sponsorship but, as well as being a fundraiser, I wanted this to be a positive experience for the youth club members that proved they could do something good for their community. I hated it when older people in the local community dismissed the young people as wee hoods, troublemakers and scum. I was well aware of just how much trouble they could make, but most of the young people I got to know just wanted somewhere to go, something to do and some hope for the future.

However, the sponsored pool tournament turned out to be a stressful twenty-four hours – eight consecutive Tuesday nights of craic and chaos in one unending day. The choice of music to play alone required all of my conflict-resolution skills.

'If yer man plays that fuckin' Erasure tape one more time I'm gonna top myself,' complained Den.

Then realising what he had just said whispered, 'Sorry, Tone. I forgot about your da. No offence, mate.'

I appreciated Den's sensitivity. This was one of the everyday phrases that pierced my heart every time I heard it now.

The daytime hours at the start of the marathon were good-natured and relaxed but as darkness descended the pool tournament became increasingly fractious. I had to break up several fights involving the cues and balls, and I had to go outside and count to ten after I discovered a series of cigarette burns on the newly refurbished pool table.

I was excited when Joan informed me proudly that the BBC had telephoned the office to ask if their mobile broadcasting unit from BBC Radio Ulster could come and do a live broadcast from the pool tournament. Some of the lads needed convincing because the BBC was part of the British war machine and they said the news was always against them. The BBC wanted to interview me and several of the youth club members live, so I agreed to speak about the project, and several of the lads promised to give a fuck-free interview. Mike Edgar and the team from Radio Ulster arrived just before midnight. At first, when they entered the smoky back room of the drop-in centre, they looked a little nervous and scanned the room for the nearest emergency exit route. They were like a media crew arriving in a war zone, but after a bit of slegging they realised our young people were only going to attack them verbally and attempt to kill them with banter.

'You're an even uglier bastard in real life than on TV,' said Soup to Mike Edgar.

'C'mon Soup, you're no oil paintin' yerself,' I said.

'Least I'm not a speccy bastard.'

The BBC team laughed and I smarted. I pushed my glasses up my nose and smiled knowingly at the broadcasters. Thankfully they were very down to earth and so they relaxed and prepared us for our interviews. I had brought my portable TV downstairs so that we could watch television and follow the telethon throughout the day. Several times that evening our efforts were acknowledged in a scroll along the bottom of the screen highlighting all the local fundraising in Northern Ireland.

'We're fuckin' famous,' shouted Billy. 'Everyone knows what we're doing the night for that big yella bear.'

'Aye, we're sittin' ducks,' warned Den, with the security implications of our widely advertised location in mind.

In those days, when a BBC channel closed for the night, the national anthem always played before the screen went to the test card of the girl playing noughts and crosses with her toy clown. And so it came to pass that just after midnight, as Mike Edgar announced that he was live from the Saltshaker Youth Club at the top of the New Lodge Road, the sound of 'God Save The Queen' echoed around the back room of the drop-in centre. None of the young people seemed to notice because they were so excited about being on the radio, but my mind was racing. If the main Provo in North Belfast was listening and thought we played 'God Save the Queen' at every youth club to indoctrinate the young people, the consequences would be terrifying. As soon as I had stuttered my way through my interview I casually shuffled over towards the television – still smiling and nodding as Den told the audience that the Saltshaker was 'class cause there's nathin to do round here and we get harassed by the Brits and all' – and discreetly switched the sound off. I thought up a story in case the angry republican arrived. I could argue that he must have been mistaken in hearing 'God Save the Queen', or maybe tell him that Mike Edgar had apologised for a technical fault with the Divis transmitter. I knew the Provos liked to blow up the Divis transmitter so I hoped this lie would redirect him to a more familiar target.

Thankfully no one seemed to have heard the broadcast but now I was feeling very stressed and exhausted. I was scheduled to take a nap between 2 a.m. and 6 a.m., with two other volunteers taking over supervision, but I couldn't sleep properly because I kept wondering what was going on downstairs. I had recurrent dreams that I was waking to the sound of the fire brigade arriving to douse the flames of the centre until the drilling of the buzzer alerted me to the fact that I was needed back at the pool table.

When I got down, there was the distinct smell of marijuana and solvents. The fire exit door was open. I suspected this was either to clear illegal odours, to enable the theft of some of the youth club equipment or to provide a secret entrance to store something illegal for a few hours. Everyone was trying so hard to look nonchalant that I knew they had been up to something. I never found out exactly what went on that night. I hope it was drugs rather than weapons. I could live with my naivety providing a venue for illicit drugs but not with being somehow party to a movement of guns or explosives that would be used to kill people. I knew that some of our young people would not contemplate doing anything like this, unless they were forced to, and most of the lads were more interested in an all-night party than a charity fundraiser. But I had also overheard enough conversations to realise that some of the young men were actively involved in the armed struggle.

To lift the mood I decided to change the music on my ghetto blaster, which I had brought downstairs from the bedsit for the day, together with all of my best albums, including Tears for Fears, Erasure, Paul Young and The Eurythmics. By 6 a.m. all that remained was my tape of Abba's *Greatest Hits Volume 2*. As far as my music collection went, the pool tournament winners really had taken it all. I just about made it to 9 a.m. and finally collapsed into bed as soon as the morning prayer meeting had finished in my office/bedroom.

Once we had all caught up on our sleep and the back room was cleaned and thoroughly aired for another twenty-four hours the event was deemed a great success by everyone. The young people had successfully completed a project that was their own idea and on top of this we had been featured as a success story on the radio. This was a new experience for our young people and they were on a high for the next few days. After several weeks of chasing sponsorship money we were able to send a couple of hundred pounds to Children in Need.

In the meantime I followed up on the other idea of a football team and secured a small grant for a football kit. I arranged for our team to play against other youth clubs in North Belfast on Saturday mornings. At first I thought the cross-community matches our team played were a good idea because the players could make friends and break down barriers. However, it soon became clear that the football pitch was just another arena for rivalry, and broken legs were the most likely outcome. The only way forward was for the young people from the different communities to play together on the same team – but no one wanted to do that.

An alternative regular soccer opportunity came via one of the 174 Trust's prayer supporters who worked at the young offenders' centre in Millisle. Every week we took a minibus to the borstal and our young people played five-a-side football against their peers who were in prison. Our players showed no prejudice or fear of the lads in prison and everyone got along just fine. A phrase I often heard was 'If you can't do the time, don't do the crime.' The youth club members treated their opponents with a mixture of sympathy for getting caught and respect for surviving imprisonment. An independent observer would probably have been surprised at the good humour and sportsmanship displayed by the residents of inner city Belfast and the incarcerated youth. I wasn't a great football coach, unfortunately, but I was very happy to take on the important job of driving the minibus and arranging for the kits to be washed every week.

I wasn't the only one making progress with marginalised youth. While I had been working with the young people in New Lodge for more than a year now, Lesley had just been successful in her application for a job with the Save the Children Fund in the Upper Shankill. She was appointed as a youth worker at St Columba's, a Church of Ireland church at the top of the Ballygomartin Road, just across the road from my old primary school. I had been unaware that Save the Children was funding work outside of Africa, in fact in the same area where I had grown up. Apparently I had been one of the children needing saved! Lesley would be running youth clubs for young people from the same estates where I had taught Sunday School and where I had worked as a van boy for the Ormo bread man for years. It was clear that there were children in need who needed saved just about everywhere. The minister of St Columba's was Rev. Tim Kinahan, who was from an aristocratic family in Templepatrick. He had recently returned from a mission in Africa and was clearly up for a challenge because the top of the Shankill Road must have seemed almost as far from his ancestral seat in Templepatrick as Africa. He got on well with Lesley even though he disapproved of her zeal for evangelism as much as she disapproved of his reverence for liturgy. They found common ground in wanting to provide youth development activities for the children and young people of the Upper Shankill.

With two salaries now in place, Lesley and I applied for a mortgage and signed up for the Co-Ownership Scheme. On the day we collected the keys of our new house in Brucevale Park from the estate agent on the Antrim Road, we walked hand in hand around the corner, through the control zone and the yellow steel barrier blocking the road, up the street and onward to our first front step and our first front door. I scanned the bricks from the ground to the roof and felt proud and elated that I now owned complete walls and a roof, in fact a whole building, or at least 50 per cent of it. We opened the new mahogany front door of our brand new luxury townhouse, entered the empty house and kissed in our new living room. This was our place now.

Later that week we asked Mo and Tonto if they would paint all of the interior walls for a small fee, which they appreciated although they went against my advice and did not declare these earnings to the dole office. In spite of their unpredictable temperaments the lads did a brilliant job and I told them they could start their own painter and decorator business and do really well. Lesley's parents were extremely generous and provided us with all the furniture we needed to get started – pine bedroom furniture, a pine table and chairs and a lovely floral sofa with matching curtains. Once all the decorating with magnolia emulsion was complete and all of the furniture delivered and assembled, it became clear that Lesley's words were true – she had made the little house lovely. The rooms were bright, in spite of the peace wall towering behind us, and the house felt bigger on the inside than the outside – a perfect TARDIS in which we could begin married life. The house smelt of fresh paint, new carpet, fresh pine and glue, presumably from the new furniture and not as a result of unapproved antics by Mo and Tonto.

We didn't believe in living together before we were married so I stayed in the bedsit while Lesley moved in, with her friend Jennifer from Bellaghy renting the spare room. I kept a close eye on the peace line so that I could be on hand in an emergency and dash around the corner should the Protestants from the other side or any barred youth club members on this side try to attack the house containing two lone Presbyterian women. Lesley was a little nervous at first but after a few weeks with no incidents she settled into our beautiful house. All of the pieces of the jigsaw were falling into place. We believed it was all part of God's plan for us and that he would protect us in our future home and in our work alongside the loyalist and republican young people that few other people could be bothered with.

'Who knows?' I said to Lesley. 'Maybe we could bring our two youth clubs together to meet each other and make friends with the other side, and have discussions with each other like they do up at Corrymeela.'

I was certain that this approach had more potential than cross-community football.

'That's a brilliant idea,' said Lesley.

9

FOR RICHER, FOR POORER

At long last it was 27 December 1986 and we were getting married. Over the past year, while I had devoted every waking hour to bringing peace to North Belfast, Lesley and her mother had managed to find enough time on top of their busy jobs to organise what they hoped would be the wedding of the year. I had received constant updates on progress on everything from flowers to venues to cars. The level of forward planning and military precision rivalled that of the ever-present British army in the New Lodge, but without the risk of anyone being shot in the back. I was aware that a few dramas had been averted en route to the Big Day, and by Christmas Eve everything was prepared for the perfect wedding, Ulster-Presbyterian style.

Apart from turning up, my only task was to organise the honeymoon.

I had also been given instructions to practise driving to the Country House Hotel in Kells on Boxing Day to ensure I would not get lost on any rural roads on the day. My limited driving and navigational skills apparently carried a high risk factor for ruining the whole day. My worst performance to date had been to take the road to Portrush (on the north coast) as the route to Lurgan (in south Ulster). Thankfully, disproving all my driving doubters, on the day itself I managed the journey admirably. Accompanied by my older brother, my best man, and an old school friend Jim, my groomsman, we arrived at the hotel in good time to check into the wedding suite, change into our good hire suits from Parsons & Parsons and get into the 1940s wedding car that awaited us for the journey to Bellaghy. As the chauffeur with an indecipherable County Antrim accent transported us through a sea of unfamiliar frosty fields I was aware that my life was about to change forever. Once the initial chat and excitement died down I gazed out the window on that crisp December morning and in the silence I experienced an unfamiliar feeling of being single and alone. This confirmed to me that I was ready for married life. More importantly, sex sanctioned by God was long overdue.

Strangers waved at our car and tooted their horns as we passed, as if we were celebrities, and there was already a small crowd assembled around the gates of Bellaghy Presbyterian church when we arrived there thirty minutes later. Getting married was like becoming a star – Lesley and I would be like Kylie Minogue and Jason Donovan for the day.

Bellaghy is a small village in County Londonderry, near Magherafelt, which at that time had around a thousand inhabitants, of which more than eight hundred were Catholics. In many ways Bellaghy was like a mini New Lodge but up the country, and with more paramilitaries and more Protestants. From this tiny population had come the great poet Seamus Heaney, two famous hunger strikers (Francis Hughes and Thomas McElwee),

Dominic McGlinchey (the best-known member of the INLA), Margaret Johnson (world-champion bowler) and Lesley Evans. Mention of Lesley's native village regularly impressed the lads at the Saltshaker. Certainly most of the residents were republicans but, unlike in Belfast, they often lived next door to their Protestant neighbours. For some reason they didn't build walls between Protestants and Catholics in Bellaghy, but everyone knew where the Protestant fields stopped and the Catholic fields started and you daren't sell your land to the other side. I was fascinated to discover how many young people in the New Lodge claimed that Dominic McGlinchey was their uncle. This heroic uncle seemed to have scores of nephews of a wide variety of ages. However the young people soon learned to temper their boasts of McGlinchey kinship when Lesley was present because she was able to verify their accuracy. My own credibility leapt considerably when I revealed on the last Tuesday night youth club before the wedding that we had received three lovely wedding presents from various members of the McGlinchey family. For some of the youth club members this was the equivalent of telling my late granny that I had got a wedding present from the royal family or the Rev. Ian Paisley.

I knew no Protestant with less hatred for republicans than Lesley. She abhorred their violence as much as I did, and had argued with her neighbours about the rights and wrongs of using violence for political ends, but she understood their point of view and regarded them as human beings she had grown up with rather than evil monsters from the other side you only heard about on TV. Lesley had grown up as an only child next door to eleven McGlinchey siblings. As a little girl her first best friend was Siobhan McGlinchey and, as they played with their dolls together, in and out of each other's houses and gardens, Lesley was like the twelfth McGlinchey. In fact there were both Protestants and Catholics standing around the church gates to catch a glimpse of the bride, although on this particular occasion Catholics were the minority. There was more to Bellaghy than labels and sectarian stereotypes – but that was true of most places in Northern Ireland during the Troubles.

At the church gates I waved at a few old school friends from Belfast who had popped up the country for my wedding day and who would be joining us later at the evening reception. I was very relieved when I got inside the church to see that all my relatives had made it to South Derry, some of them in a specially hired minibus. Bellaghy was only a thirty-minute drive from the city but up the country always seems very far away for Belfast people. The road from Belfast up the country is always longer than the same road home. Rev. Kinahan arrived wearing a pure white clerical vestment embroidered with golden sacred symbols from his time in Africa. The look of surprise on some of the faces at the church gate suggested that the people of Bellaghy thought the Pope had arrived – some were pleasantly surprised and some were appalled. Bellaghy Presbyterian was between ministers at the time so my minister, Rev. David Temple from Ballygomartin Presbyterian, who had been supporting my mother through her grief, conducted the wedding ceremony while Rev. Kinahan said the prayers. A concern whispered at the back of the church that 'yer man's goin to do a Hail Mary, so he is' was unfounded.

The music was led by two of my favourite women in the world. The organist was Ruth Hutchinson, my former P5 teacher who had been my friend and an exceptional encourager ever since I was eight years old, and the soloist was my mother's dear sister, my Auntie Dot, who was a talented singer and the warm heart and sense of humour in our family circle.

I kept looking around to check if my mother was okay because she was clearly up to a hundred. I sat at the front beside my best man and groomsman as my younger brother and Lesley's cousin's son William ushered in the guests. I fidgeted, checked I had the ring, turned around to smile and wave at friends, and sweated and fidgeted and in my nervous state, it even crossed my mind to wonder what I would do if Lesley didn't show up like in all the best soap operas. Ruth kept jooking over her reading glasses towards the back door until, to my great relief, she started to play the 'Trumpet Voluntary' and then the processional hymn 'Love Divine, All Loves Excelling'. I turned around and there she was, my Lesley, in a wedding dress and veil looking beautiful, sparkling and smiling her perfect smile. I unexpectedly felt very emotional and, as the congregation stood to sing, I had to choke back the tears. The bridesmaids followed behind as Lesley's tall father led her elegantly up the aisle. When she arrived beside me I told her she was beautiful and held her hand, which was shaking a little, in my hand, which was sweating a lot. When the music stopped, the congregation sat down and, after a moment of dramatic silence, the wedding ceremony began. My mother was audibly distraught for most of the service and some of the congregation also became distraught at her distress. At most weddings the mother of the groom shed a little tear as she let go of her son, but at my wedding my grief-stricken mother sobbed for the loss of her husband who could and should have been sitting beside her and holding her shaking hand. I was upset but I was determined that my father's absence was not going to dampen my big day. Within a few minutes we had completed our 'I wills' and 'I dos' – no 'to obeys' – and we headed into the minister's room to sign the register and make it official. At this point Auntie Dot sang an uplifting version of 'Down from His Glory' to the tune of 'O Sole Mio'. When we returned hand in hand to the front of the church, as Dot sang her heart out in the final verse, my best man nudged me from behind and asked if I wanted just one Cornetto.

When we processed out of the church it seemed as if half the village was waiting to throw confetti at us. As a native of Belfast it was a new experience to be in a public place and to have strangers throwing material at me that wasn't intended to cause injury. We began our journey to the Country House Hotel in Kells in our classic car. This was not the same village of Kells as in the world-famous multi-coloured *Book of Kells* although as a village the County Antrim Kells did contain a remarkable number of purple Presbyterian hymnbooks. This was our first private moment since being declared man and wife and we chattered like breathless and excited children the whole way to the wedding reception. Lesley kept asking me if I liked her dress and if her hair was okay and I told her she was perfect. Now it was just the two of us, together, forever.

Arriving at the hotel we thanked God that it wasn't raining as usual or snowing as we prepared for the all-important wedding photographs. My new wife encouraged me to relax and smile and not to stand like a model in a Club Book. Lesley's mother later sent the best photographs to the *Ulster Tatler* magazine and they were published, although the editor did have to request that at least one should include the groom. Ultimately the dress, the flowers and the photography were independently judged a great success when Lesley was awarded runner-up in a bride of the year competition.

As the guests arrived for the reception and the congratulations and kisses and hugs continued my face ached from smiling so much for the first and last time in my life – empirical evidence that this was indeed the happiest of days.

The speeches passed off with some sadness due to my father's absence, some nervousness on my father-in-law's part, a reminder to all present by Rev. Taylor that they needed to be saved and numerous embarrassing references to my poor driving skills. Lesley and I were determined that our evening reception would not be a traditional Ulster wedding disco at which elderly relatives danced with small children to 'The Rivers of Babylon' or 'Blanket on the Ground' performed by a cabaret band from Ballymena. Earlier in the year we had spotted a group of young saxophonists busking in Belfast city centre. Buskers were cutting edge in Belfast in 1980s – anyone playing musical instruments outside BHS or Marks & Spencer was at risk of being blown up by a 1000lb car bomb planted by the IRA. For years the only common street music in Belfast city centre had been a flute band or the music from Mickey Marley's Roundabout. While other shoppers passed by and threw coins into their woolly student hats, Lesley approached Saxophone Madness and asked them to play at our wedding reception. Most of our generation had their first dance to Chris de Burgh's 'Lady in Red', but our first dance was to Glenn Miller's 'Moonlight Serenade'. The only problem was that two hours of Glenn Miller wasn't as effective as 'Dancing Queen' at getting people of all ages up on the dance floor.

However it was a happy evening with friends and family, apart from when I persuaded my mother up for a dance. She was very happy for me but as I held her I could feel her sadness. A sea of sympathetic faces surrounded us as we waltzed around the dance floor reminding everyone of how beautifully my mother and father had danced together.

We tried to speak to everyone to thank them for coming and for the lovely presents. Eventually, as Saxophone Madness repeated 'In the Mood' for the third time, Lesley and I left in the Renault 5, which had tin cans tied to the back bumper and confetti scattered all over the blue bonnet. We returned to the back entrance of the hotel five minutes later and secretly crept through the kitchens to spend our first night in the honeymoon suite. After twenty-three years of waiting, I was definitely in the mood.

The next day we made our way to the airport and flew from Belfast to Heathrow and then on to Casablanca where we got stuck in fog and nobody played it again for Sam. As we waited in the airport a tall Englishman in our travel group took the lead in representing the concerns of the delayed British tourists.

'I recognise him,' said Lesley. 'Is he from Bellaghy? Does he know Mummy?'

I looked closely at this distinguished-looking gentleman until finally the penny dropped.

'It's yer man that does that new Oprah show on BBC1 in the mornings,' I exclaimed.

'Oh my nerves!' cried Lesley in a barely controlled whisper. 'It's Robert Kilroy-Silk!'

Eventually we boarded our flight to Marrakesh. Robert Kilroy-Silk's commanding presence proved useful when we finally arrived late at night and he took charge of the drop-off of exhausted tourists from our package holiday coach to the assigned hotels. I wasn't sure which fact was the hardest to take in – that we were married, that sex was now permitted, that we were in North Africa, that there were camels outside or that I was on honeymoon with Robert Kilroy-Silk.

When we finally arrived at our hotel in the middle of the night I was disappointed to find that our room contained twin beds instead of a double. I attempted complaining to reception that this was inappropriate bed layout for a newly married couple but with limited shared language skills it was difficult to get to the bottom of such a complex cultural issue with the Moroccan gentlemen on reception. We had to settle for pushing the twin beds together. This was unfortunate as we had enough to figure out without the added hazard of falling down between the two beds. After waiting so long for sex I felt that the very least we deserved was the space in which to try to do it properly. However by the end of the week we had attempted every possible angle and had eventually worked out how everything fitted together. As the days went by in Marrakesh I swaggered a little every time I remembered the night before and the fact that I was now a fully experienced man of the world.

For ten days we were in paradise and a world away from peace walls and petrol bombs. This was my longest consecutive series of days in more than a year in which I hadn't been called a speccy bastard. Of course I felt guilty about who was opening and locking up the youth club while I was watching snake charmers and belly dancers. I felt guilty about how my mother was surviving her first New Year's Eve and New Year's Day as a widow while I was enjoying a North African New Year's feast that cost £100 a head – more than the cost of forty variety meals from Kentucky Fried Chicken – and watching even more delightful belly dancers, albeit furtively so as not to upset my new wife. A few minutes after midnight, Lesley and I walked hand in hand into the garden of our hotel in Marrakesh. We stood in silence beside the pool surrounded by palm trees and gazed up at the magnificent and clear Arabian sky. Then we kissed and embraced. It was perfect.

'They're looking up at that same sky and those same stars back in Belfast,' I said romantically.

'Let's forget about Belfast tonight', said Lesley.

After ten days of souks, sand and sex, and several offers of a camel in return for my new wife, we headed home. Back at the airport we picked up our car and we drove back to Belfast for our first night together on the peace line. It was cold and frosty on the broken pavements at Brucevale Park and all was quiet. We caught red-handed two of Lesley's student flatmates – both called Heather, both from Portadown – putting rice in our bed and cling film on the toilet as a cheeky welcome home. After hugs all round they scurried off chuckling and I carried Lesley over the threshold into our house.

10

IS THERE ANYBODY THERE?

'Is there anybody there?' whispered Lesley, anxiously scrunching up the top of the brand-new wedding present duvet with both hands.

I was in my pyjamas, motionless with fear and peeking out of our small bedroom window to see what was happening at the back of the house.

'I can't see anyone,' I whispered tensely.

It was our first night together in the house. I had woken to the sound of shouts and footsteps but I couldn't work out how close they were. At first I lay still, trying to stop myself breathing so that I could listen for the tiniest sounds to help me to assess the level of danger. Was a burglar trying to break into our house? Was someone about to rob us of all our wedding presents? Of course they would do very well with our new video recorder, matching kettle and toaster, and impressive collection of Ainsley Country Garden porcelain, but they would probably leave my model Dalek behind. Surely if they had any sense and professional acumen they would have carried out a burglary while we were still thousands of miles away in Morocco rather than upstairs in bed. After lying in bed paralysed by fear for a few minutes I got up to investigate, accidentally waking my new wife in the process.

'No, I don't see anyone,' I whispered, 'I think we're all right.'

'Are you sure?'

'Yes. There's no one there.'

'You're scaring me,' said Lesley. 'I never heard much noise at night here when it was just me and Jennifer.'

'Sorry, I just want to be sure,' I said, scanning the cats' home, the perimeter of the army base and the other side of the peace line. Nothing moved. I started to breathe normally again.

It was never completely dark at the back of the house because the huge security spotlights around the border of Girdwood barracks cast a blurry orange glow that created quasi-daylight on even the darkest of nights. This made it impossible to achieve complete darkness in the bedroom, even with the curtains closed, but at least it was easier to see what was going on at the back of the house in the middle of the night. I opened the bedroom door, crept down the stairs and checked the front door. The telephone was in the front hall if an emergency call was required. After a few minutes of careful surveillance I slipped back into bed and embraced my anxious wife. I prayed silently that God would protect us from harm and keep us safe until morning.

'We're all right,' I said and eventually we tired of listening for fresh and suspicious noises outside. Exhaustion replaced fear and we fell asleep in each other's arms. Little did I know that this was going to be the first of many such nights. I was constantly alert to the many threats, real, possible and imaginary, all around us. The regular nighttime incidents would begin when I wakened with a start at some noise outside. The waking, the listening, the checking, the watching all became routine. Normal people put their cat out every night. We checked our security. I fitted extra locks on all the windows and doors although my limited DIY skills meant that these added security measures were unlikely to protect us from a serious attack. I had made my bed and I was going to have to lie in it.

I was a new husband and I felt that it was my responsibility to protect my wife. A lifelong commitment to pacifism didn't equip me to win a fight to the death with an intruder with a handgun – I would have to use my head to escape any danger before coming face-to-face with any balaclava-ed attacker. Vigilance was essential at night on Murder Mile. I had no idea whether we were in grave danger or at no risk at all. Perhaps the Protestants who attacked our houses would spare us if they found out where I was from, or maybe they would target us for the treachery of living with the other side. Perhaps the Provos had decided we were harmless Christians and off limits for a republican attack. Or maybe they had decided we were legitimate targets for trying to persuade young people not to engage in violence. The threat to our lives was out there in the darkness – or not. I trusted God to look after us but I was scared too.

Ivan Martin and Richard Young on Downtown Radio woke me up at 7.30 a.m. that first morning and immediately I heard activity in the tiny kitchen below. When I wandered downstairs I saw my brand-new wife busily setting out brand-new placemats, knives and spoons for breakfast on our brand-new pine dining table. It was a long time since I had entertained the thought of a weekday breakfast. In the bedsit I was usually so tired from working the night before that I skipped the first meal of the day, preferring an extra half-hour in bed to any form of sustenance. No doubt this unhealthy habit had contributed to my suspected stomach ulcer.

'Oh, I'm sorry – I won't have time for breakfast. I need to get round to the office.'

Lesley was walking towards me carrying a tray of fresh toast and boiled eggs. A look of disappointment crossed her face.

'Are you not having a proper breakfast?' she asked, genuinely shocked that I was prepared to start the day on an empty stomach.

'No, I don't really have time for breakfast, except at the weekends,' I explained.

'But I've to go to work and I'm very busy too and I got up before you just to make it for you,' replied Lesley.

It was typical of Lesley to get up early especially for me. She always went out of her way for me. This was the orderly family breakfast she had grown up with in Bellaghy. She felt that a good wife should make her husband a good breakfast every day, and that a good husband should sit down and eat it and appreciate it. As I kissed Lesley on the cheek before leaving the house I noticed a look of hurt on her lovely face. I felt a pang of guilt that she was already being a better wife to me than I was being a husband to her.

At lunchtime every day we ate together – I walked home from the centre and Lesley drove back from Springmartin. Our little hatchback was getting on a bit now, but it was still running well, although starting to rust around the bottom of the doors, a problem probably brought on by our trips back up to the salty air of the beach at Portstewart where we had walked hand in hand as students a few years before. Some of the youth club members had kindly offered to set fire to the ageing car so that we could both claim on the insurance and get compensation from the Northern Ireland Office for a Troubles-related attack, but I politely declined.

I knew of very few working couples that could have lunch together nearly every day and it was a special hour for us in the midst of our busy schedules of youth clubs, trips and funding applications. Lesley's work with young people in the Upper Shankill estates was going very well although she had to contend with several members of the church who were outraged that she was allowing raucous teenagers to walk on 'holy ground' (through the church vestibule) en route to the church hall for a game of Unihoc. Our lunchtimes together were an oasis of calm in the middle of every day. We had a snack and a chat and we watched a new Australian soap opera called *Neighbours*. As the months went by, we followed the ups and downs of her young people in the Shankill, my young people in the New Lodge, and Des and Daphne and then Scott and Charlene in Ramsay Street.

After a few months we decided that we wanted another little creature to care for together. We bought a Japanese lionhead goldfish and named him Aslan in a nod to C.S. Lewis. We loved Aslan, but you couldn't cuddle a goldfish, and a baby was out of the question on the peace line, so we decided to buy a dog instead.

I had a poor track record with pets, with a high body count, but Lesley was good with animals. So we scoured the ads in the Pets' Corner of the *Belfast Telegraph* until one day we saw a litter of wire-haired fox terriers in Ballysillan. We called the owners, made an appointment to see the pups and fell in love with the runt of the litter, a cute little scamp with an underbite. We named her Fara after the place where Noah was born in the Bible, because she left floods everywhere but most people thought we had named her after one of Charlie's Angels. We took her for walks in the Waterworks and up the Cavehill. There was drama when she came off the lead, ran on to the Antrim Road and head-butted an Ulsterbus, appearing to be dead but coming round miraculously, like Lazarus, in the emergency vets on the Shankill Road. Then on the Twelfth of July she ran away on a visit to Bellaghy and came home with a smile on her face. She delivered a litter of puppies eight weeks later. Our beloved pet shared our desire for good cross-community relationships. Unfortunately one of our neighbours was a grumpy old man who hated dogs, especially Fara, who occasionally chose to slip under the fence to shit on his petunias. He complained regularly about her and referred to her as 'your fuckin' mutt'. One day I received a phone call from the Shankill Leisure Centre to inform me that our dog had been found wandering in their car park, over a mile away from our house and across two major road junctions. I wondered how on earth Fara had managed this trek. The mystery was solved later that day when one of my youth club members turned tout and told me that he had witnessed a grumpy old man coax Fara into his car before driving off in the direction of the Shankill Road. Our neighbour had kidnapped our dog and dumped her on the other side of the peace line. We turned the other cheek, pretended nothing had happened and offered to pay for a new fence to protect him from our fuckin' mutt. And we kept Fara well away from his petunias. However after this incident I wondered if the symbolism behind this nasty act was that my neighbour would really like to dump me back on the Shankill Road where I belonged.

On our first Eleventh Night in the house it was very hard to get to sleep. While the bonfires lit up the sky over North Belfast we decided to go to bed early, and hope and pray for the best. The disturbed sleep that followed was inevitable. We were wakened by the sound of Fara barking and scratching at the back door.

'Is there anybody there?' asked Lesley as she sat up in bed.

A cat or a rat or a gunman might have disturbed Fara. At least now we had a guard dog – well, a small alert dog – but she punched well above her weight in terms of the noise she made. I was standing in my boxer shorts peeking out of the bedroom window.

'Is there anybody there?' repeated Lesley.

Nights in our bedroom were starting to sound like a séance.

I could hear the distant sound of people on the other side of the peace line singing 'The Sash' interspersed with closer shouts of 'Kick the Pope!', 'Kill All Taigs!' and 'No Surrender!'. I could hear bricks and bottles landing ever closer to Brucevale Park. Our homes were the nearest and easiest targets to attack as a celebration of my culture. Perhaps the noise I'd heard was a wee hood about to throw a brick or a petrol bomb across the peace line.

'I think they're all still up at the boney across the road,' I whispered. 'I think we're all right'.

Once again, after a few minutes of careful watching I slipped back into bed and hugged Lesley, who was so used to this kind of night now that she had already fallen asleep. I prayed my usual prayer: that God would protect us from harm and keep us safe until morning.

We had a regular stream of visitors to our home, although a few people declined our invitation to visit in case their car got hijacked or damaged. Some were in awe that our commitment to peace and zeal for God were such that we were prepared to come and live here, while others thought we were not near wise in the head. The young people from the youth club would call in for a chat regularly too, although we had to establish some boundaries after Lesley pointed out that I seemed to spend more time with the youth of the New Lodge than with her and that our living room, our only room downstairs, was not a youth club.

'Lads, I only want youse callin' round in an emergency or if we arranged it, now I'm married and all, and you're not allowed to smoke in our house, okay?' I explained to a group of the lads.

'Aye, Tony thinks he's a big lad now he's nat a virgin no more,' commented Soup. 'Only sleggin'!'

However when the young people called around they were always very respectful of our home. Thieving bits and pieces from the drop-in centre was acceptable, but stealing from our home seemed to be regarded as out of bounds. That was until Lesley's glasses went missing. It was, after all, the 1980s, when glasses were big and bold. With her keen sense of fashion, Lesley had the very latest bright red plastic glasses, which she used for watching television and driving, as she was only slightly short-sighted. For months she searched for them, trying to remember where she had put them, until the day there was a rap on the front door.

'Here, Tone,' said Den, his eyes shifting from side to side to check if anyone was watching, like a member of the French Resistance in *'Allo, 'Allo.*

He took a small shiny object from his pocket and handed it to me quickly. 'It's a comm from Seamie in the Crum,' he said, and ran off in an instant.

Seamie was one of the occasional youth club members who was currently incarcerated. A 'comm' was the term for a secret communication from a political prisoner that had been smuggled out of the prison by insertion into one of the orifices of a visitor. They were usually written on wafer-thin cigarette paper or torn off Gideon Bible pages, then rolled up and covered in foil. I opened the secret message quickly, wondering why Seamie had chosen to communicate with me in such a clandestine manner and slightly concerned that what I was doing was unintentionally illegal. Then when I thought of the way that comms usually made it out of prison, I had an urge to wash my hands even more quickly. The comm from Seamie was written on a very thin piece of paper, from the edge of a page of the Bible. I was doubly troubled that I was in receipt of an illegal communication and that in spite of all our chats about God, Seamie had chosen to tear up his prison Bible to write secret messages rather than read it to discover the Message. I unfurled the tiny scroll and read: *'Dear Tony, I'm sorry for stealing Lesley's glasses. I needed them for disguise. Sorry mate. Seamie.'*

Seamie had bright, almost fluorescent, ginger hair. I wondered how he could possibly have imagined that wearing bright red women's glasses would have provided him with some form of camouflage. The fact that the message was coming from inside the prison suggested that his disguise hadn't worked. I was annoyed that Seamie had abused our trust. We had welcomed him into our home and he had stolen Lesley's glasses. However I appreciated the sincere apology while washing my hands again and again for the next few hours. When I showed Lesley the contents of the message she rejected the idea of demanding the return of her spectacles. With only one possible delivery method, she was unlikely to want to put them back on again anyway.

A few weeks later there was more furious knocking on the front door, which Lesley answered.

'Let me in, Lesley, the fuckin' Brits are after me!' shouted an out-of-breath and red-faced Mo.

'No way!' said Lesley. 'You're not hiding in here.'

'Let me fuckin' in, ya bitch,' he roared.

'No way!' repeated Lesley. 'Hide in your own house.'

Lesley was braver than me. I would have let him in. Mo had no idea there was more to Lesley than fashion and fun. She was not to be underestimated. Mo looked disgusted, spat in Lesley's face and ran off. I ran after him and eventually caught up with him at the top of the New Lodge Road. It seemed that I was having more luck in catching him than the Brits.

'Take your glasses off, Tony,' he said helpfully, not wanting to damage my spectacles in the street fight he was anticipating.

I wanted to call Mo a cocky wee shite and give him a good

slap he would never forget. But here I was, a lone pacifist on the wrong side of the peace line. I'd never struck any one in my life and he was a street fighter who would surely knock my melt in. I controlled my rage at him for spitting on my wife and told him he was big disappointment and a coward for being abusive to a woman. I was shaking with rage but I just walked off. When I returned to the house, Lesley was upset and still crying, more at the insult than the spittle.

'What did you do?' she asked.

'I told him he was big disappointment and a coward for being abusive to a woman.'

Lesley looked at me, as if to say, 'Is that it?'

There was a line between turning the other cheek and being a doormat and I think I was on the wrong side of the line from my spouse's perspective.

A few weeks later I was once again wakened from a light peace-line sleep by the sound of bins clattering, running footsteps and shouts at the back of the house. Had someone thrown a brick or petrol bomb at the wall of the army barracks? Was this the beginning of a mortar attack? Were we about to become collateral damage?

'Is there anybody there?' asked Lesley wearily as she turned over to try to get back to sleep.

I could see a group of soldiers running along the back of the houses, hurdling all the fences, en route to our slighter higher fence, erected to protect Fara from our neighbour's hatred of Protestant mutts.

'There's a man,' I said in astonishment.

All these nights of checking and there had never been anyone there before.

'What?' cried Lesley

'There's a man!'

'What do you mean, there's a man?'

'There's a man!'

After nightly enquiries for months upon end neither Lesley nor I could believe that I was answering in the affirmative. Had someone, somewhere decided that we should be killed tonight? I was supposed to protect her in these circumstances but what use was a pacifist husband if someone was attacking our house, I thought. I couldn't even react appropriately to swearing and spitting. Directly below the window I could see the outline of a man and I could see and hear him trying to open our back door – turning the handle and pushing the door with his shoulder. Fara was barking ferociously and I could hear the sound of her leaping up and down on the other side of the door.

Suddenly the troop of soldiers came charging towards our back yard and the man fled in an instant, hurdling over the rest of the fences and off towards the safety of the New Lodge. I ducked down so as not to attract attention from the gun-toting soldiers. Once the commotion had passed I went downstairs and comforted Fara with a pat and a Bonio. When I returned to bed, to my surprise, Lesley started to laugh.

'What are you laughing at?' I asked.

'At long last, somebody was there,' she replied.

And we'd survived, I thought to myself with relief.

11

PEACE IN THE REAL WORLD

I wasn't stupid. I knew peacemaking wasn't going to be easy. But I had no idea it was going to be as hard as this. Lesley reminded me constantly that I was taking everything too seriously. She advised me to try to find a way of switching off from work and encouraged me to take up a new hobby. My model Dalek had been completed and painted long ago, so I started to think and dream about how I might try to pursue my interest in broadcasting while working on the peace line at the same time.

The violence continued on a daily basis. The IRA was excelling at murdering policemen with booby-trap bombs. Whether the lethal device was hidden behind a hoarding, in a bin or in a briefcase, the deadly impact was the same. The Provos were terrifyingly skilled at carnage by this stage and so proud of themselves. Not only were they completely right about everything and absolutely justified in taking every life, but now they were killing people with flair and expertise. The loyalist paramilitaries never had the same finesse, and simply murdered people as punishment for being born Catholic. They also continued their habit of shooting Protestants who they thought sounded or looked like Catholics. Meanwhile the Irish National Liberation Army and Irish People's Liberation Organisation were so committed to feuding with one another that they were murdering more Catholics than Protestants. The British army denied the existence of a shoot-to-kill policy, but nonetheless shot and killed a lot. The bloodletting and the tit-for-tat butchery were terrible. Most people said it would never end, and the two sides seemed further apart than ever.

What difference could a few naive Christians on the peace line make in the midst of all of this slaughter, I sometimes asked myself, after hearing the latest news headlines. Many of the young people in the youth club seemed to enjoy the drama and excitement of the Troubles, even though their family and friends were victims of the violence. The youths came along to the evening clubs every week and those who were unemployed – which was pretty much everyone who had left school – dropped in regularly to our daytime unemployed club. Soup and Billy were there nearly every day and they knew we would support them with whatever issues they were facing in their lives. But as far as breaking down barriers and promoting peace went, we were barely scratching the surface. Few people in Northern Ireland seemed to feel any inclination for compromise anyway. The politicians defended their own sides and the churches buried their own dead. I was constantly disappointed that most of the churches had chosen to comfort their own rather than promoting peace and turning the other cheek. The Protestant churches had failed to apply their renowned theological rigour to the words in the inerrant scriptures which said love your enemies. Meanwhile the Irish Catholic bishops were maintaining a breathtaking hostility towards even the tiniest steps towards integrated education. I was still inspired by a Jesus of Nazareth who said we should forgive a person seventy times seven – 490 times more than the average Belfast churchgoer ever managed. We were able to forgive our own side's wrongdoing and jump on any scrap of evidence to prove that the other side was unforgiveable. To suggest you might forgive your enemy was seen by your own side as unforgivable too. The softness of love and forgiveness was swamped by the desire to win a long war that no one was ever going to win. There were a few brave and inspiring clergy who took risks for peace and reconciliation, but they were never remotely mainstream. Although they were role models for me, they were just about tolerated by their churches but not always by their congregations. I believed I was in some ways following in their footsteps, albeit without the restrictions or protections of a dog collar. I tried to preach the message of reconciliation to the young people in the youth club but it felt like I was teaching starving people how to use a knife and fork properly when they were more worried that someone was stealing all their food.

'It's war, Tone,' was the answer to everything.

For young republicans the validity of the armed struggle seemed beyond question. There were also serious risks in making any negative remark about the IRA in this part of Belfast. This narrow view of politics reminded me so much of the attitudes on my side. Our prejudices about the other side were taught to us by our own, and rarely challenged by a different viewpoint let alone an actual experience or conversation with 'themuns'. Northern Ireland spawned no great inspiring cross-community leader for peace and non-violence, and there was no mass movement for peace and reconciliation from the ordinary people. The Peace People of the 1970s were by now a distant memory that only served to prove that mass peace rallies could not stop the killing. Most people just kept their heads down, blamed a minority on both sides for causing all the trouble and tried to live as normal a life as possible under what the British government had called 'an acceptable level of violence'. Not one death was acceptable to me. I struggled most when young people in the youth club cheered at the death of an enemy. One minute they were ordinary teenagers, happily playing a game of pool or slagging Big Mickey for being turned down by a beautiful girl, and then news came through of the death of a policeman or a British soldier and they roared for joy. I never hid my disgust when this happened and challenged the young people every time. They always responded that I was too Christian to understand the realities of war and too Protestant to understand that their suffering under the British war machine justified the celebration of death. George Seawright was a loyalist politician who talked about burning Catholics and he was no hero of mine, but when the young people jumped up and down to celebrate his shooting I felt sick to my stomach. It seemed to me as if part of their humanity had died, or had at least been anaesthetised, for the sake of the great cause.

The wider world seemed uncertain too. There were plans to build a huge tunnel under the Channel to connect the UK and France. The talk in Belfast was that it would never work. Meanwhile scientists reported a hole in the earth's ozone layer over Antarctica. The only way to stop this was for us all to stop using deodorant sprays in our oxters. I dreaded to think of the smell in the back room of the Saltshaker Centre during the summer scheme if Lynx deodorant spray was banned. The talk in the pubs of Belfast was that stopping spraying would never work anyway. Mr Gorbachev was bringing *glasnost* and *perestroika* to the Soviet Union and was starting to unfreeze the Cold War. However, Rock Hudson's death from AIDS, the *Challenger* disaster and the explosion at Chernobyl certainly hadn't made the new world order feel any safer.

Then I unexpectedly found inspiration in *Witness*. The fact that Han Solo/Indiana Jones appeared in the movie was enough to convince me to watch it but in the first few minutes it became clear that this was not a science fiction blockbuster but an unusual crime thriller, set in the Amish community of Pennsylvania. It tells the story of an Amish boy who witnesses a murder in the men's room in a train station in Philadelphia. Harrison Ford is the police officer assigned to the case and the plot thickens when the boy identifies another police officer as the killer. In the end Harrison Ford, the boy and his mother are all under threat and hiding away from the killers in the Amish community in Lancaster County. I had never heard of the Amish before this movie. So, just when I was struggling to maintain a commitment to pacifism against the backdrop of seemingly unstoppable violence and churches that were lukewarm on peacemaking, here was a Christian community completely and unequivocally opposed to any violence of any sort for any reason. This was a refreshing change from the widely held belief of a 'just war' in Christianity. I was struggling with the whole idea that killing human beings could ever be 'just' and I questioned why so many Christians believed that God was always on the side of the country they happened to be born in.

The Amish are a peace-loving community of farmers who believe in complete separation from the world. They wear simple clothes, travel in horse-drawn buggies and centre their lives on family and church. I'd never seen anything like it. The Amish have suffered for their belief that all violence by anyone in all circumstances is wrong. They ended up in Pennsylvania because they had to flee persecution in Europe for refusing to fight in wars. All of this was new and inspiring information to me and presented most pleasantly in the shape of Kelly McGillis as the Amish heroine of the movie. In the Irish churches all that 'love your enemies' talk didn't get very much attention but Amish people didn't just talk about love and forgiveness and turning the other cheek – they practised it. They went to prison for refusing to fight in wars. Here was a movie about Christians who shared my beliefs about guns and violence and yet they didn't seem judgemental and self-righteous. Not long after I watched the movie, we received a letter at the 174 Trust asking if we would be interested in hosting a Mennonite volunteer for two years. We often hosted volunteers from England, but these young graduates tended to have recognisable evangelical credentials. Our most recent volunteer was Big Dave from Birmingham, a Cambridge graduate with a big heart for the poor and homeless. He was the most radical Christian I had ever met and also my first vegetarian friend. Big Dave really put his faith into practice, although his patience and respect for Ulster Presbyterians wore very thin the more he got to know us. Once the young people accepted that he was not a poorly disguised British soldier-spy, they loved him.

After some research I learnt that Mennonites were Anabaptists and pacifists just like the Amish, but a different branch that wore normal clothes, had cars and phones and were much more engaged with the world. In fact Mennonites were so committed to involvement in the world that they sent missionaries all over the globe, not to save the natives like Presbyterian missionaries, but to work alongside local Christians to promote, peace and justice and reconciliation. So we discussed the volunteer application from a Mr David Moser from Indiana, earnestly looking for signs in his personal statement that he was well saved. His credentials in peacebuilding and youth work were impeccable but he had not used much of the language we looked for to indicate he was a good sound evangelical rather than a dodgy liberal who might not believe that Jesus had actually walked the earth. In the end we had to assume that this young Mennonite from Indiana was in fact a bona fide Christian and, sure, once he arrived we could either work on getting him saved or send him home.

On the day our American volunteer arrived I was assigned to collect him at the airport. It turned out that I was about to meet my best friend in life. In 1987 jade was the latest colour for the fashion-conscious male in Belfast. The era of tartan patterned jeans had passed and I had recently bought a pair of jade trousers, a jade and white striped shirt and matching jade and blue shoes from John Frazer's in Gresham Street. When I saw David Moser I was amazed at how tall he was at 6 foot 7. He was wearing a checked shirt and jeans and he looked and sounded like an elongated John-Boy Walton. Dave was equally amazed by how green I was. It was as if he had been met at the airport by a green leprechaun. In the excitement of meeting him and chatting about life in Indiana and Belfast, I made one of my typical driving errors on the way back from the airport by veering on to the wrong side of the road.

'Holy cow!' he exclaimed.

I had never heard anyone use this phrase before, apart from Batman. I told Dave that I was just trying to make him feel at home by driving on his side of the road for at least a part of the journey. After all his months of preparation, and presumably concern from friends and family back in Indiana regarding his safety, it would have been tragic for him to perish in a car accident with a wee green man within an hour of arriving in the country. It soon became clear that this was an even Bigger Dave than Big Dave from England, even taller and with even more radical views about peace and love and forgiveness. David Moser was a man whose faith I had doubted based on all of my own prejudices and my narrow view and experience of Christians outside of my Ulster evangelical bubble. When we swiftly became good friends I had to make a confession.

'Dave, do you know when we got your application,' I said sheepishly, 'I was worried that you weren't a real Christian. Now I'm wondering if I am a real Christian.'

Dave laughed and gave me a big hug.

'Holy cow!' I said in a bad American accent.

I figured this was what instant forgiveness felt like.

The young people in the youth club loved this Bigger Dave even more than Big Dave and decided – due to his great height and facial hair – to name him Chewbacca.

Once David Moser had settled in, I invited him to come with me to a church conference to which I had been invited to talk about the role of the churches in peacebuilding. These conferences were well-meaning, theologically correct, profoundly aspirational but generally resulted in very little action. I was certain my Mennonite friend would rock the boat with a well-educated perspective and an engaging humility that would be hard to dismiss. Once the conversation began it didn't take long for some of the delegates to shift uncomfortably at some of Dave's views about really loving your enemy and turning the other cheek, not just spiritualising it or finding complicated theological get-out clauses for not doing what Jesus said. One woman in our seminar seemed to feel personally insulted by the concept of Jesus the pacifist.

'Well, that's all very well, but you have to want to be forgiven before you are forgiven. You have to repent of all your sins before our Lord Jesus Christ.'

Dave listened and acknowledged her point and tried to understand her views. He didn't argue with her and she seemed to find this disconcerting. I felt this woman was no stranger to a good argument. I noticed a vein in her forehead started to throb.

'Well, that's all very well, but it couldn't happen here,' she posited. 'We are under attack from terrorists every day.'

I think this woman lived in a detached cottage with a rose garden in the wealthy village of Hillsborough rather than on the peace line so her use of the word 'we' was a bit of stretch.

Dave continued with a calm explanation of the outworking of a Christian commitment to non-violence. I wanted to cheer him when he answered each criticism with a clear, convincing alternative viewpoint.

'Well that's all very well, but what do you do with the murderers in your wonderful community in Indiana? How do you deal with killers in your town? Do you just forgive them and let them go free?'

Dave thought for a while and then answered, 'My grandpa told me there was once a murder in our town a long time ago'.

This alone suggested that pacifism was working in their part of the world.

'There was this guy travelling through and he killed a man at the gas station.'

The murderer wasn't even from the town! The commitment to non-violence was so embedded in his community that a murder (by an outsider) was a rare and distant memory. This made it even more remarkable that Dave had come to live on Murder Mile in Belfast.

The vein in the women's forehead throbbed again. Dave humbly devastated the argument with simple facts. This was my kind of Christianity. I wanted more of this, please. But there were no Mennonite Churches in Northern Ireland. I suppose pacifist Christianity has never been too popular in these parts. After all we are known across the world as the country where Christians kill each other over religion.

The more I saw violence on the streets of Belfast, the more I saw hatred in the eyes of our youth and the more I heard words of war and vengeance, the more convinced I became that pacifism was the only way. So with my new American brother-in-arms (or rather totally-opposed-to-arms) at my side I continued on the path of peacemaker. No matter how difficult or seemingly impossible our dream for peace, Dave gave me the courage and support I needed to keep going.

12

BLESSED ARE THE PEACEMAKERS

'Here comes the God squad,' guldered Tonto.

We were out for a Sunday afternoon stroll through the Waterworks, passing other dog walkers, skinheads and a few alcoholics, when a group of our faithful youth club members spotted us. The teenagers often referred to the staff and volunteers as the God squad and it was one of my favourite insults. As I walked with Lesley, Dave Moser and Fara by my side I felt like we were the peace squad, although obviously with none of the military paraphernalia associated with an actual squad.

'Is Big Lesley pregnant yet, Tony, ya boy ye?' asked Mo with a filthy chuckle.

This was followed by a group chant of 'yeoooooo'. The teenagers' fascination with our sex life had almost disappeared now that we had one, but at times the fact that we were no longer virgins was a vein of comedy too tempting to resist.

One of the great benefits of slegging was that it made it impossible for me to take myself too seriously.

'If you read the subtext of the "Genesis of the Daleks" episode of *Doctor Who*, Soup, you will see a parallel with war and peace in the world today,' I once earnestly explained. 'Do you want to borrow the video?'

'Wise up, Tone. *Doctor Who* is a loada shite for borin' wankers,' replied Soup.

'I'm only sleggin', Tone,' he added, every time an insult stung me.

A bit of mockery did me no harm at all. In fact, the saplings of spiritual and social smugness, which had been growing within me largely unchecked for years, were regularly hacked down on the streets of North Belfast.

'But God wants you to wait until you're married because your body is a temple of the Holy Spirit,' I once told a discussion group of sexually active teenagers.

'Wise up, mister. Youse Christians are all Holy Joes and head the balls that just can't get bucked,' advised Colette as she twisted pink chewing gum around her forefinger. This time no one said she was only sleggin'.

For most of my time working and living on the peace line there was no shortage of humour and lightness, and there were even glimmers of hope. North Belfast might have consisted of two separate communities, but both were full of strong caring families, and people with a dark sense of humour who didn't take life too seriously – apart from religion and politics of course, which were more important than life itself. Fear and frustration were not my dominant emotions during the time I spent on the peace line, and this is testament to the warm nature of the people who lived there. I met many, many good people and I could count the psychopaths on one hand – the same hand one of them once threatened to cut off. In spite of the violence and hatred that stained our souls, a solid humility remained in the hearts of many of the Belfast people.

I had heard about a charismatic Christian community that met in another little house on another peace line around the corner in Duncairn Gardens. They were called the Lamb of God Community and they were much more ecumenical than the 174 Trust, with several Catholic sisters and the odd priest fully involved. Although a few of my colleagues disapproved, I decided to go to one of their prayer meetings because I believed that the opportunity to pray with Catholics on the peace line was a rare gift. Most evangelical Protestants were against praying with Catholics – it was regarded as joint worship and this was forbidden because it was seen as encouraging them to 'persist in the deep theological error of the Mass'. I was never quite so sure that you could avoid praying with Catholics because I could be standing next to a Catholic at a bus stop on the Antrim Road and the Catholic could be praying silently at the same time as me and God was probably listening to my 'Lord's Prayer' just as much as he was hearing their 'Our Father'. I knew that God might be pleased to see the two sides praying together in spite of all our differences. When I arrived at the prayer meeting I was a little nervous because the more ecumenical types like them tended to disapprove of the more evangelical types like me. There was even them and us at a prayer meeting. However I was given a warmer welcome than I could have imagined. More nuns hugged me in the first five minutes than I had met in my entire life. This was an older generation of Belfast peacemakers who had been quietly praying and working for peace in North Belfast for years. During Lesley's work in West Belfast she had linked up with a similar group at the Cornerstone Community on the Springfield Road, and she talked about meeting an inspiring Catholic priest, Father Gerry Reynolds, who radiated the peace of Christ. These small groups of humble Christian people were often at the centre of the suffering: visiting those who had lost someone as a result of violence, and at the heart of quiet and sometimes secret efforts to begin dialogue between enemies throughout the Troubles. These were the Christians on the margins of their churches, quietly bringing compassion in the midst of the trauma but at the same time taking risks to talk to the perpetrators of great suffering.

'This is Tony, Sister. We've been praying together,' said one kindly nun with a Southern accent to another elderly nun at the end of the prayer meeting, 'Sure, he's a lovely rapport with the Lord.'

As I got to know these Catholic brothers and sisters I was amazed to discover that they regarded me as a bona fide Christian in spite of the errors of my church, which was a mirror image of what I had been taught about them at my church.

Another member of this inspirational band was a woman called Margaret Wilkinson, a very wise retired missionary who was on the board of the 174 Trust. Margaret Wilkinson had served God for many years as a Presbyterian missionary in Southern India. She was one of a group of dedicated women who had worked with Amy Carmichael, a heroine of the Irish Presbyterian overseas missions. After decades in India working in partnership with all of the other churches to help the poorest people in towns and villages, it was the most natural thing in the world for Margaret to work in partnership with Catholics to address the social needs of the most disadvantaged people in Belfast. Obviously this didn't go down well with the more conservative Presbyterians, especially when she joined a new ecumenical community in North Belfast called the Columbanus Community. Although, perhaps because of her age, her gender or her shining faith, they didn't attack her as much as you might have expected. Of course, I loved her. Here was a diminutive single woman in her seventies coming back to Belfast after decades in India, and challenging the religious and political status quo with faith, grace and gentleness. When she noticed Lesley and I were exhausted, Margaret gave us the keys of her apartment in Castlerock beside the sea and we had a weekend break away from all the tensions in Belfast.

For months Lesley and I had been discussing how we might bring the young people from our two youth clubs together so that they could become friends and understand each other better. We knew we would have to be careful that everyone was safe and that the event didn't turn into a riot. I knew from the cross-community football that bringing enemies together to compete was not a good idea. A few of the young people had visited each other's clubs or bumped into each other at our house, but we needed a good number to agree to meet together for a meaningful encounter. Lesley and I agreed that if the young people had never met one of the other sort before it was essential that they had a positive first experience. We had heard stories about a charity that organised holidays where a Protestant and a Catholic were twinned and stayed with a family in the USA. If the two teenagers bonded it was a great success and they even kept in touch when they got home to Northern Ireland. But if they didn't get along they came home hating the other side even more, because they didn't like the only one of the other side they had ever had to live with. We needed to find some neutral and accessible territory where all the young people would feel safe.

We realised that the Columbanus Community would be perfect. Of course, Margaret Wilkinson was delighted and offered a few words of wisdom to temper our overenthusiasm. She invited us to visit the community, which was located in a huge mansion, about one mile up the Antrim Road, in a mixed middle-class area where the IRA shot at judges. We checked out this location with both sets of interested young people and all of them were happy with this neutral place that was 'full of Holy Joes from both sides'. Most of the young people in both youth clubs declined the invitation to meet the other side but, as the paramilitaries on both sides didn't forbid the venture completely, we ended up with a group of about six teenagers from each club. The stage was set for real peacemaking. Not just Lesley and me trying to convince one side that the other side wasn't so bad. This was giving the young people an opportunity to find this out for themselves.

We read some books from Corrymeela about helping groups to talk to each other. Then we planned what to do. We agreed to play some teambuilding games to help the young people to get to know each other, to facilitate a short discussion about what they wanted to know about each other and, if there were no casualties by this stage, to finish with tea and biscuits. The young people from my club were aged between sixteen and eighteen, while Lesley's were between thirteen and fifteen. They had grown up a couple of miles apart but they might as well have lived on different planets. They lived in separate streets, went to different schools and played different sports. One of the most striking experiences of living on the other side was that it showed me how ignorant the two sides were about each other. So many myths and stereotypes had been passed down the generations in the two parallel universes on either side of the peace walls that it was hard to know where to begin to replace prejudice with reality. When everyone arrived Lesley and I welcomed the other club especially warmly to show that they were humans, although Gerry whispered just loudly enough for me to hear that because I was from 'up there' I was probably 'on their side'. The two groups sat down at opposite ends of the room. My lads were quite boisterous and were slegging each other as usual, but Lesley's group were more awkward. The teambuilding games helped to break the ice and some of Lesley's kids started to laugh at the banter from my crew, especially when everyone introduced themselves. When Billy said his name, Den joked that with a name like that he was in the wrong group. Billy smarted a little but accepted the ribbing. The Springmartin boys loved this and it helped everyone to relax much more naturally than our teambuilding games. Nonetheless the two sides remained at their own end of the room.

Next came the discussion where they were going to respect and forgive each other and realise they were all the same and want to meet every week to work for peace. Lesley and I took a big flip chart page each and wrote at the top:

What do you want to know about Catholics?

What do you want to know about Protestants?

After an initial silence the two groups started to shout out a few questions and some of the young people wrote down their own. Of course the questions included 'Who wants to lumber big Lesley?' and 'Why is Tony such a speccy bastard?' but the young people also asked some good questions which they had never had an opportunity to ask directly before. They had learned all about what the other side believed from their own side, so there were a few surprises, especially when the members of one group did not have a unified view in response to each question. This immediately killed off the prejudice that 'themuns is all the same, so they are'.

Lesley's group asked my group why they couldn't accept that they were British.

'We're not British, we're Irish'

'No you're not, you're British'

'No we're Irish, so we are!'

'You're British. This is the UK!'

'Irish! *Tiocfaidh ár lá*!'

'British!'

'Irish!'

'British!'

'Irish!'

My group asked Lesley's group, 'Why don't you believe in Mary?'

Few of the young Protestants went to church and they didn't know the answer.

My group asked Lesley's group, 'Why don't you want a United Ireland?'

'Because we're British, we're not Irish'

'No you're not, you're Irish'

'No we're British, so we are!'

'You're Irish. This is Ireland!'

'British!'

'Irish!'

'British! No surrender!'

'Irish!'

'British!'

This British/Irish debate was getting us nowhere. It reminded me of the *Monty Python* sketch in which the opposing characters continuously slap each other across the face with a wet fish, although this conversation was clearly less funny.

Lesley's group asked my group why they wanted the Brits out.

At this point Gerry gave the young loyalists an Irish history lesson covering five hundred years of British oppression, which left them speechless.

'Why do youse march through our areas? Why is that your culture?' asked my group.

Lesley's group clammed up completely. This seemed the appropriate moment to draw attention to the fact that both groups had posed the question, 'Would you have sex with someone from the other side?' This provoked laughter, a few dirty jokes that seemed inappropriate on the premises of the Columbanus Community and a definite sense that the answer to the question was yes.

'Hands up anyone who has lost a family member or a friend in the Troubles.' said Lesley.

Every one of the young people put their hand up. This felt like a turning point and the mood improved a little. After the discussion most of the young people shook hands and said they wanted to meet again before giving each other a light, having a smoke together and returning home in their separate minibuses. My minibus was jubilant – concluding that Protestants were ignorant and didn't know their own history and were afraid to argue their point because they knew they were wrong. Lesley's minibus was angry that they couldn't compete with the knowledge of the other group.

'Lesley, we felt wick, so we did. They know everything about their history and politics and we know fuck all.'

Lesley and I agreed that the cross-community session would have worked better if her group had done some preparatory work beforehand. If they had explored and understood their own history and culture a little better, then they would have been able to engage more confidently with the others. This later became known as 'single identity' work; later still, single identity work also became a convenient way of securing funding with no intention of ever meeting the other side.

On the way home in Lesley's minibus there had also been a much freer discussion among her young people over the hypothetical question of whether they would be prepared to 'fuck a Fenian'. Apparently the conclusion of this conversation was that love, or at least sex, could conquer all.

13

APPRENTICE DJ

I had been worrying about my media career for a while now. Of course, I was sacrificing it for the sake of God, peace and the unemployed youth of North Belfast but I had not completely let go of my broadcasting aspirations even though the BBC had turned me down. I wondered if this rejection might have been as a result of my voice – very few of the presenters I heard on Radio Ulster in those days spoke with a normal Northern Ireland accent. They talked about 'Ulstah' and 'Nawthawn Ahland' and interviewed very clever people who adored 'the awts' and celebrated that latest triumph at 'the theatah'. The presenters at Downtown Radio, Northern Ireland's only commercial station, didn't sound local either – more mid-Atlantic, which was odd as most of them came from County Down – but the station did have a lot more listeners.

As a young man I had been a devotee of BBC Radio 1 and Radio Luxembourg, but Downtown had always been the local radio station of choice in our house. My parents rarely tuned in to anything else, apart from the British army frequency to find out where a bomb had exploded or which roads were blocked.

Downtown Radio was as distinctively Northern Ireland as potato bread and petrol bombs. It was the only local radio station with commercial breaks and it seemed to me that the whole broadcasting operation was paid for by adverts for Martin Phillips Carpets and Ferguson Flowers. I had spent most of my school years being driven to school to the sound of Ivan Martin and Richard Young's breakfast show during the week and enjoying an Ulster Fry at the weekend accompanied by Big T, Derek Marsden and Candy Devine. Big T was the biggest country and western presenter not to come from Nashville and he exclaimed 'Yes indeedee' almost as often as he played Philomena Begley records. My late granny had treasured the signed photograph of Big T that sat on her mantelpiece describing him as 'a lovely big fella with his moustache and all'. Candy Devine was a big and beautiful kaftan-wearing Australian singer, with a voice that made me feel like warm chocolate was being poured slowly into my ears. Candy had moved to Northern Ireland in the 1960s and had ultimately become the broadcasting mammy for the whole of Northern Ireland. Her best and most accurate jingle was 'She's so sweet, she's so fine, Candy Devine'. Such were the advances in technology that listeners could phone Downtown Radio with a request and Derek Marsden would play their granny's favourite song live on the air on his very own organ within minutes. Derek Marsden also played hymns on a Sunday morning to a huge audience, and delighted the believers of Mid Ulster by playing Rev. William McCrea singing a country gospel version of 'The Old Rugged Cross' in an American accent.

The combination of Willie McCrea's Free Presbyterianism

and DUP unionist politics was music to the ears of the County Antrim Bible belt, although Daniel O'Donnell's version of 'What a Friend We Have in Jesus' brought a certain cross-community balance. The presenters on Downtown Radio were household names and local celebrities in Northern Ireland. If you managed to get Big T to open your church jumble sale you were lucky indeed. By 1987 Downtown Radio had re-branded as DTR FM and was playing the latest hits as well as a selection of songs invariably described as 'an oldie but a goodie' to attract a younger audience as well as grannies listening on AM and country and western aficionados from Portadown. The radio station, based in the Kiltonga Industrial Estate in Newtownards, produced a remarkable variety of specialist programmes on the arts, sport, folk, rock and gospel. This was all every impressive, but as a young and trendy evangelical Christian I was aware that Downtown Radio did not yet have a 'rock gospel' programme. I was a member of the Word Record Club, which sent me a featured 'Contemporary Christian Music' album every month. These were usually very well produced by American singer-songwriters such as Larry Norman, Amy Grant and Steven Curtis Chapman, whose music was a good as anything on Radio 1 but with a focus on loving God rather than your girlfriend. DTR FM was trying hard to appeal to a younger audience but their gospel music programmes, although very popular, featured a selection of music that I considered old-fashioned and embarrassing. So I decided to write a letter to John Rosborough, the Head of Programming, to suggest a programme called *Rockspel* which would be a clever combination of rock and gospel, and not embarrassing at all.

I was about to leave the house for a busy day of assisting with job applications in the unemployed club and submitting funding applications when I noticed a letter in a Downtown Radio-branded envelope lying on the welcome mat. Fara was sniffing it curiously.

'Les!' I cried excitedly.

Lesley emerged from the bedroom with a half-made-up face and joined me at the front door where I stood with the white envelope in my hand.

I took my time opening it. I was preparing myself for either great disappointment or the beginning of my trajectory toward Oprah Winfrey-scale success. Fara could tell this was a crucial family moment and scratched at my calves with her paws. I took a deep breath and opened the envelope. John Rosborough was inviting me to Downtown Radio with a selection of my rock gospel albums. He wanted to record me introducing a few tracks to hear what I sounded like on the radio and to get more of a sense of the programme I was proposing. Lesley hugged me, I kissed my lovely wife, and Fara, sensing the excitement, peed on the carpet.

A few weeks later I arrived at the security gate of Downtown Radio with an armful of LPs and a well-rehearsed script for a fifteen-minute pilot recording of *Rockspel*. John Rosborough met me at reception and welcomed me with the smooth voice that I knew well from his *Take it Easy* programme. I was soon to learn that the other presenters called the Head of Programming 'JR'. To all aspiring DJs, this man had all the power of a Dallas oil baron, although he was a much nicer person than JR Ewing and, unlike the country and western DJs, I never once saw him wearing a stetson on the Kiltonga Industrial Estate. On this debut visit JR ushered me into the Downtown Radio record library, which was filled with shelves and shelves of thousands of 33s and 45s, and which smelt of cigarettes and vinyl. I was surrounded by decades of the best selection of pop and country music that had entertained the population of Northern Ireland since Downtown Radio was launched in the 1970s. I wanted to search every shelf for rare and beautiful records, like Frida from ABBA's solo albums. It was hard to believe that I was actually standing in the heart of the music. I could not have been further away from unemployment and intimidation and insults on the peace line. My father, for years the DJ at the Westy Disco, would have been so proud to have seen me standing there, on the cusp of becoming a professional DJ on his favourite radio station. He used to scorn the English-based BBC stations he heard me listening to, mainly because they never gave traffic updates for Northern Ireland. But with Downtown Radio you were always certain to be kept abreast of heavy traffic at the Sandyknowes Roundabout at Glengormley. I was about to have a once-in-a-lifetime opportunity to become a famous presenter on Downtown's hallowed airwaves. After a tour of the gospel music section in the library, which mainly consisted of country and choirs, JR led me down a corridor towards the studios with their large heavy padded doors. We passed the news booth where at that very moment, live on the air and right in front of my very eyes, a newsreader was informing the whole of Northern Ireland about who had been shot dead at their front door that day. I could see a telephone sitting on the padded desk in front of the newsreader and realised this may well have been the actual phone the IRA called with their coded bomb warnings. We passed the main studio where a red light indicated a live broadcast was in progress. When I peered through the window I was excited to see the famous face of Big T smiling and smoking. It was hard to believe that I was within feet of a radio star just as he was probably saying into the huge microphone in front of him some famous words like 'Yes indeedee, righty doo, and here comes Hank Williams just for you.' I was already nervous at the thought of my imminent audition but my close proximity to a major celebrity set my heart racing.

We entered a small recording studio through another set of heavily padded doors. In front of us was a console of lights and buttons as impressive as the bridge on the *Starship Enterprise*. There were two shiny steel turntables on either side of a mixing desk and large cassette machines with oversized cassettes marked 'jingles' located above the control panel with indicators showing the sound levels. I began to understand that they used this state-of-the-art equipment along with every conceivable muffling material from floor to ceiling to achieve the perfect FM sound quality I had experienced on my radio for years. John told me to take my time and get myself organised and I took a few deep breaths to calm my nerves. He would cue up the music on the turntables and all I had to do was speak without stuttering. I handed him my sample albums by Amy Grant, Cliff Richard and Stryper – a heavy metal band whose lead singer screamed about Jesus instead of Satan. The first track in my pilot was to be 'Jesus Makes Me Wanna Sing' by Stryper.

'Hello and welcome to *Rockspel*, with me, Tony Macaulay here on DTR. Gospel music like you've never heard it before!'

Cue Stryper heavy-metal guitar intro.

John Rosborough listened carefully as the pilot proceeded but gave nothing away. I couldn't tell whether my audition was going well or as badly as my audition at the BBC a few years earlier, when they had laughed at my mispronunciation of Maghaberry. JR wasn't laughing at me, but he wasn't giving me any positive feedback either. After recording the pilot segment he thanked me politely and ushered my back up to reception, just as the real live Candy Devine was arriving in a beautiful kaftan with an armful of LPs. Candy smiled and said hello. She was every bit as big and warm in real life as she sounded on the radio. Now I had met a star, albeit briefly! I couldn't wait to tell my mother. I was certain that this would cheer her up, although she would also know that this new career would have made my father incredibly proud, so it would probably upset her even more in the end.

'Have you pitched this to anyone else?' asked John Rosborough seriously as he bade me goodbye.

'No,' I replied.

His expression didn't change at my response, but I was hopeful that he was thinking that he might need to snap me up quickly before the BBC could spot my great potential.

I heard nothing for weeks. Sometimes when I was on duty in the back room of the Saltshaker, when I should have been concentrating on trying to win at least one game of pool against one of the lads, or keeping an eye on the fire exit door to ensure the contents of the tuck shop were not being removed under my nose, I daydreamed of a telephone call from John Rosborough offering me a series. Then, inevitably, my mind would go to the negative place that assumed that nothing this good would ever happen to me.

Eventually one evening I was outside the house, busily washing the Renault 5 and trying to stop Fara from barking at passing soldiers, when Lesley ran out.

'It's John Rosborough from Downtown Radio on the phone,' she gasped. 'Oh my nerves!'

I dropped my chamois and the bucket and tripped over Fara as I ran toward the telephone in the hallway. Lesley stood close beside me, trying to listen in.

'Congratulations, Tony,' said JR. 'We'd like to offer you a pilot show.'

I calmly accepted the offer and thanked him politely for believing in me and took a note of the practical details of what would come next on my journey to the airwaves. As soon as I hung up Lesley and I hugged and jumped up and down so boisterously that we scared Fara and she hid under the stairs. Perhaps dreams could come true. Maybe I could make a difference on the airwaves if not on the streets. I could bring to the people of Northern Ireland songs of love and peace and reconciliation and God would use me as a messenger of Good News to help bring an end to all the fighting. As I gushed out all of these thoughts and dreams Lesley hugged me and advised me to calm down and keep it in perspective. I phoned my mother immediately.

'Guess what?' I said proudly.

'What's wrong?' she asked.

Ever since my father died my mother assumed every phone call was going to be more bad news.

'Nothing's wrong,' I said. 'It's good news for our family for a change.'

'What?'

'You're speaking to the newest presenter on Downtown Radio!'

'What?'

My mother cried with a mixture of joy and grief and I promised to call over later to tell her all about it. When I arrived, everyone in the family and half the street had already been told about my exciting news.

14

IN SICKNESS AND IN HEALTH

'Get back into bed, Tony,' said Lesley in sleepy exasperation.

'I thought I heard something round the back,' I whispered, predictably.

'It was probably a cat again or your friggin' snoring!' replied my love, as she turned her back on me to return to sleep, 'There's never anybody there!'

I was standing in my Nick Kamen boxer shorts checking out the possible dangers lurking down below at the back of the house. Maybe Lesley was right; not about my snoring of course, but it was possible that the noise was nothing but a cat fight. I was exhausted by this nightly security check. A full night's sleep was a rare luxury. Lesley was correct – for a year now there had been only one attempt to breach the security of the house and even then we were almost certainly an intended escape route rather than prospective victims of a sectarian attack. I had invested in even more extra locks for all the doors and windows, although my DIY skills were such that they offered little effective protection. I seemed more scared than my wife and it wasn't supposed to be that way round, although she had lived in a republican area all of her life and I was still getting used to it. I had only been threatened a few times since I started working in the Saltshaker but nothing serious. The worst was a solvent abuser threatening to smash in my speccy face because I had banned him from the youth club for sniffing a furniture polish aerosol in the toilets, which I warned was not only damaging his health, but also his relationship with God and the ozone layer.

The combination of long working hours and lack of sleep was once again having an impact on my health. I was constantly recovering from the flu or a cold and Lesley had started to join in the extended snuffling. One morning Lesley awoke with a heavy cold and decided to stay in bed for a rest.

'I'll see you at lunchtime,' I called as I dashed downstairs. 'It's the prayers for healing this morning!'

Then Lesley developed eczema on her hands and even I realised that it must be stress-related. We needed to take action to look after ourselves otherwise we would be of no use to the people we were trying to help. We hadn't taken a proper holiday since our honeymoon – just a few weekends in Bellaghy and a bank holiday Monday in the rain in Portstewart – so we decided that a fortnight in the sun was exactly what we needed. When I told the members of the Tuesday night youth club we were going abroad on holiday the news elicited a range of responses.

'Ah, you and big Lesley deserve a wee break,' said Soup.

'Yousens must be fuckin' loaded,' exclaimed Paddy.

In reality we weren't earning enough money for a fortnight in Benidorm but I managed to find us a late deal to Greece in the window of the Co-op Travel Shop. Lesley couldn't understand why the holiday was so cheap but I assured her that I had bagged us an outstanding Aegean bargain. According to my atlas and my understanding of the prevailing winds in the past year, Halkidiki was far enough south in Greece to be safe from the nuclear fallout from Chernobyl. We booked two whole weeks off work and arranged cover at our youth clubs and volunteers who would take the youth club keys to check for intruders during a break-in because the police would assume any reported break-in was a trap to kill them. Big Dave agreed to both fish- and dog-sit for us, and to keep an eye on the house because half the youth of North and West Belfast were aware that it would be temptingly empty.

The holiday was a welcome break from work but it rained the whole time, the apartments – which were located three miles from the nearest shop – were still under construction, and we ran out of money after ten days. While the builders drilled outside and the thunder roared overhead Lesley read a few novels and copies of *Hello!*, and I read the biography of Martin Luther King that Big Dave had recommended. I was more inspired than ever by this courageous peace-builder who believed that love was stronger than hate, and that light was more powerful than darkness. The biography was a huge hardback book that had weighed down our suitcase considerably, but the terrible weather provided an opportunity to study the life of a hero of Christian pacifism at a time when I was living and working in the midst of a senseless spiral of tit-for-tat violence. Here was a man of faith who stood firmly by nonviolent principles as a way of challenging discrimination and securing civil rights.

'Where is the Northern Irish Martin Luther King?' I wondered.

I was disappointed when I read about Luther King's marital infidelity and the pain this caused his wife but then I realised that my hero was not a faultless man. Every day I was absorbed and nourished by powerful words: 'Returning violence for violence multiplies violence, adding deeper darkness to a night already devoid of stars. Darkness cannot drive out darkness: only light can do that. Hate cannot drive out hate: only love can do that.'

'This man was incredible,' I cried as I turned the pages describing his turning the other cheek under great provocation.

I cried when I read the chapter about his assassination.

'This book is brilliant!' I kept saying to Lesley during the many hours I spent reading within the confines of our sparsely furnished room in our unfinished apartment block. Lesley was a bit quiet.

When we arrived back in Belfast we were shocked to discover that there had been a break-in at the house. Dave had forgotten his keys one day and had been forced to break a window to get in to comfort a fretting Fara. It was ironic that after all of my months of worrying about a possible forced entry by a sectarian hood, the only incident of breaking and entering involved a Mennonite pacifist from Indiana. We didn't even have any photos of our Greek holiday – when we returned home we discovered that the film in Lesley's camera had not been properly inserted. We rowed about whose fault it was, and neither of us spoke a word through a whole Sunday afternoon omnibus edition of *Eastenders*.

Eventually we kissed and made up, in spite of the fact that all of the lovely photos of the apartments being built, the orange trees on the dusty road outside the building site and the beauty of Mount Athos peeking through the rainclouds were lost forever. Later that month I brought my own camera to the Saltshaker Pensioners' Club to take a few pictures of the senior citizens for the newsletter. I had a few exposures remaining in an old roll of film, which included a few photographs of my father's final day out – an Easter Monday trip to Ballycastle the previous year. I was going to take the final few shots, post the film off to be developed and then find an appropriate moment to give my mother the final photos of my father to keep as a happy memory. I set the camera down on one of the tables to help several elderly ladies down the step at the front door, but when I returned my camera was gone. It had obviously been stolen but I optimistically created a poster asking for the missing camera to be returned, explaining that there were photos of great sentimental value on the film. Of course I never saw the camera again and the final photographs of my father were lost forever. I was getting sick and tired of all of this. In fact I was sick and tired a lot of the time. Sometimes Fara hid in her bed to get away from the sounds of petrol bombs and even Big Dave got depressed when one of the young people he had been making real progress with let him down. No one turned up for the cross-community meetings. I couldn't tell whether it was forbidden by the paramilitaries or just so boring as to attract zero interest. During the last youth club trip to Greenhill YMCA in the Mourne Mountains I had had to clean up vomit from all over the bunk beds due to the abuse of several smuggled bottles of vodka. It seemed that no one was interested in God or peace or love. Maybe my head was indeed in cloud cuckoo land after all.

Even our first family gathering in the house was a sad occasion. Lesley and I provided the tea and sandwiches after my father's inquest at the Crumlin Road courthouse because we lived just around the corner. It was like a rerun of the funeral but with greater emphasis on the method and details of the suicide. This was the last thing my mother needed. This process, in full public view, in the grand surroundings of the courthouse, in front of an authoritarian-looking judge was a good top-up for her feelings of depression and loss, and reminded her just how traumatic the events of the previous year had been. I visited my mother as often as possible to see how she was coping. She was attending a day centre for people suffering from depression and was receiving counselling at home by Cruse, the bereavement charity. All of this helped but it couldn't bring my father back. A few days later Lesley arrived home from a particularly difficult day at work just as I was leaving to visit my mother.

'I'm just popping up to see how Mum is doing. I'll be back soon,' I said as we passed at the front door. We were like ships in the night.

It was Remembrance Sunday and I had skipped church because I had become increasingly uncomfortable with the connection between church and state at these services. For as long as I could remember, the Remembrance Day service was the most well-attended church service of the year in Ballygomartin Presbyterian Church. At Easter there were the same few people in the congregation, at Christmas the back rows filled up, but on Remembrance Day there weren't enough seats for everyone. Remembering our war dead attracted more Ulster Protestants than the birth, death or resurrection of the Son of God. This confirmed to me that my people, who always talked about being 'For God and Ulster', were ultimately always much more for Ulster than for God. Big Dave explained to me why Mennonites did not have Remembrance Day services and how they had gone to prison as conscientious objectors for refusing to fight in wars. Every year at the Remembrance service I would wear my poppy and stand during the Last Post and the minute's silence remembering all the lives that had been wasted in all of the wars in this sad world. I asked God to take away our violent human nature and prayed for an end to wars and for peace in my land. However I was certain that God was not British and that we were not completely justified in the taking of every life on behalf of our state in the history of the world. For months now I had heard about and experienced some of the more shameful actions of the British army on the streets of my city and I felt uncomfortable with the Union flags and with singing 'God Save the Queen' during the church service. I wondered if Catholics hung Irish tricolours and sang 'The Soldier's Song' in chapels at Easter, but I was pretty sure they didn't or I would have heard all about it. As far as I could understand from my reading of history, the Christian church had always been at its most brutal, corrupt and anti-Christ when it had been appropriated by the nationalism, politics and power of any country. So I was enjoying a rare heathen lie-in that Sunday morning when there was a news flash on Downtown Radio. News was coming in of a terrible bomb attack at the Remembrance Sunday service at the cenotaph in Enniskillen. There were reports of many people killed and injured. I heard interviews about people bleeding, buried and dying on a street in Enniskillen at a religious service on a Sunday morning. I felt physically sick. This feeling of being so sickened that I could feel it in my guts was becoming more and more familiar to me. I phoned Dave Moser and advised him not to walk along the streets alone that night in case of any random drive-by retaliatory sectarian attacks and, sadly, my prediction of such attacks proved to be justified.

I already knew all of the well-worn justifications for this barbarity that I would have to listen to in the days ahead. My pleas for pacifism would just be pissing in the wind. However in the midst of the pain and suffering in the days following the atrocity, the justifications and condemnations, an unlikely hero emerged. In the history of Northern Ireland, Gordon Wilson of Enniskillen is one of very few people remembered as a man of Christian faith who spoke words of forgiveness in the midst of violence and hatred. The BBC interviewed Gordon Wilson and he spoke with great clarity and dignity about the loss of his beloved daughter Marie, who held his hand and told her father she loved him before she died underneath the rubble. When speaking about the killers of his daughter he said, 'I bear no ill will. I bear no grudge. Dirty sort of talk is not going to bring her back to life.' Gordon Wilson was on every news bulletin around the world for days. This extraordinary man, who had suffered inconceivable loss, showed the world, not anger, bitterness and intransigence but love, peace and forgiveness. He gained respect across the world.

The only voices I heard raised against Gordon Wilson were those of the nastiest unionist politicians who wanted a carpet-bombing of South Armagh and West Belfast to wipe out the IRA, and presumably everyone else living in those communities. In the youth club the justifications of the bombing were more muted than usual. Some of the young people said it was a mistake and a few said quietly that it was wrong. No one criticised Gordon Wilson although I did have a few challenging exchanges.

'It's war,' said Gerry predictably.

'Two thousand years of British oppression,' added Paddy.

'Do you honestly think that killing more people like Marie Wilson is going to bring you a united Ireland?' I asked.

'It was a British army target,' said Gerry.

'But she wasn't a British soldier,' I replied.

There was silence.

'And what would happen if you forgave the Brits the way Gordon Wilson is prepared to forgive the IRA.'

'Never!' said Gerry.

'Never?' I asked.

'Never!' he repeated.

'Now you're starting to sound like Ian Paisley,' I replied.

'What the fuck do you know about the sufferin' of the people round here anyway. Sure you're only here to preach at us,' said Gerry, getting genuinely angry now.

I knew it was better to stop the conversation at this point.

In spite of all the tension, violence and intimidation, we had succeeded in establishing a small cross-community oasis in the heart of republican North Belfast. We had Protestants and Catholics working together on the ACE Scheme and across the peace line. We even had Darren and Roberta, who were from loyalist areas, working in the café, and everyone got along really well most of the time, even when the toasties were burnt. However in the days following the Enniskillen bombing I seriously wondered if I was wasting my time. I talked a lot to Dave and together we supported each other to keep going in spite of our growing sense of despair.

Not long after the bombing a group of the lads from the youth club arrived at my house and I invited them in for a cup of tea. It seemed like a good opportunity to try to be a positive influence but I noticed Lesley flinch when the group came into the living room. The group stayed for a couple of hours, chatting, slegging and discussing music, religion and politics in a friendly manner. It was one of those occasions when I thought I might not be wasting my time after all. When the group eventually departed I noticed Lesley wasn't happy.

'What's wrong?' I enquired.

'I wanted a night off,' she said. 'I've been working with young people every night this week too and I need a break for one night in my own house.'

'But is this not what we're here for?' I said. 'We had a really good chat with the lads tonight and I think it shows we're making a difference in their lives. They really need someone to listen to them. Someone who cares about their lives.'

'But what about me?' said Lesley.

'What do you mean?'

'What about me?'

'But you're okay, aren't you?'

'Of course I'm okay – living here on the peace line, you up and out of bed every night, getting used to being married and looking after you every bloody day, and working long hours in my own job, which is just as important as yours, by the way.

'What about me?' she repeated. 'You're more interested in saving the world and looking after those wee lads and your mother and any stranger that walks through the door of that Saltshaker but what about me? Who's interested in looking after me?'

'Me, of course,' I said.

'Well you wouldn't think it.'

Lesley began to cry and I felt terrible. She always listened and took care of me. This was our first proper married row that was not about something trivial like my bad driving or Lesley spending too much on nice clothes. Our raised voices sent Fara scurrying to her bed. I felt guilty. Here I was trying to bring peace to Belfast and failing miserably and in the process causing arguments with my wife in my own home. Once I stopped being defensive and we had both calmed down we agreed to spend more time together, just the two of us. We planned to return to the Country House Hotel in Kells for one night for our wedding anniversary and put into practice everything we had learnt since our bedroom fumbling in the same spot a year earlier. We agreed to have 'Lesley and Tony nights' when no one else would be allowed to interrupt us, not even Rev. Taylor. We couldn't afford to go out much but we went to the cinema and to Kentucky Fried Chicken in Glengormley where we regularly shared a bargain bucket in the car park. On our days off we returned to Portstewart where we had first fallen in love and we went for long romantic walks along the beautiful beach. Margaret Wilkinson let us stay in her flat in Castlerock for a quiet weekend away from the peace line. Back in Belfast at weekends we treated ourselves to a night in front of the television laughing at *Cheers* on Channel 4 with a Chinese takeaway from a hot food bar on the Cliftonville Road that did lovely sweet and sour pork.

15

MURDER MILE

I vowed never to eat another sweet and sour pork ball in my life. The food poisoning was so debilitating that I had already spent three days in bed. The January weather was dull, I was sick and tired, my peace building was going nowhere, my father was still dead, my mother was still heartbroken and my wife wasn't happy. It was not a good start to 1988. And then it got much worse.

Lesley had persuaded me to try some tea and toast so I was sitting up in bed with a plastic floral tray on my lap watching the news on the portable TV in the bedroom.

'Reports are coming in of a shooting in North Belfast ...'

I immediately felt on edge.

'Police say that in the past hour a nineteen-year-old man has been shot dead in the New Lodge area.'

New Lodge? I hadn't heard the shots so it couldn't have been close by. Nineteen? Instinctively I did a roll call in my head of all the members of the youth club who were nineteen, hoping and praying that all our young people were safe. Usually in these circumstances your worst fears were not realised and it turned out that the victim was not someone you knew personally, but every so often very bad news followed about a friend of a friend or a family member. This was everyday life and death in Belfast.

I heard an urgent rap on the front door of the little house and the sound of Lesley rushing to answer it. I knew immediately something was seriously wrong.

'Is Tony in?' said Gerry.

'Thank God it's not Gerry!' I thought.

'Yes, he's upstairs in bed. Still sick with the food poisoning from the Chinese. Are you all right, Gerry?'

'I need to talk to him.'

'Go on up.'

Gerry was always pale faced, but when walked into the bedroom that day his face was ashen and his cigarette-holding hand was shaking. I felt a sickness in my stomach more profound than any symptom of food poisoning. I knew right away why Gerry was here. I just didn't know the details yet.

'Who is it?' I asked. 'I heard it on the news.'

Gerry sat down on the edge of the bed. 'It's Billy,' he said, looking down at the floor.

I felt as if I had been thumped in my poisoned guts.

'No! Are you sure?'

'It's Billy,' he said. 'He was lyin' sleepin' on the sofa in his house and the bastards burst in and shot him in the chest.'

We sat in silence for a minute, both trying to take it all in. We were in shock but while I was teetering on the path to despair, Gerry was getting dangerously angry.

'After all the fuckin' harassment,' he seethed, with hot tears on his cheeks, 'they wouldn't leave him alone.'

'Now Gerry, don't you be goin' out doin' anything stupid the night,' I said.

'What about the fuckin' bastards that done this?'

'Well, they will have to stand before God …' I knew I sounded sanctimonious and useless.

'What if I don't want to wait for that? No one's gonna listen to all your forgiveness crap now.'

We sat in silence for another few minutes.

'Do you want to pray?' I asked.

'Yes, Tone.'

I prayed a short simple prayer for Billy's family and friends, for safety for Gerry and all the young people in the youth club, and asked God that Billy's killers would be brought to justice. All I could do was listen and pray and encourage Gerry to look after himself. Lesley had been listening at the door and came in with more tea and tears in her eyes.

'It's awful,' she said. 'Are you sure it's Billy? This is terrible.'

Billy had always been fascinated by Lesley and Lesley flirted with him a little because it was easy to make Billy blush in spite of himself. Lesley hugged Gerry and told him to look after himself. We chatted for a while about what a good mate Billy was, about the loss of his father in the McGurk's Bar bombing, the impact of this on his poor mother and on all the lads in the youth club. It was so unfair. His life had been difficult enough and now it had been taken away from him, brutally and in an instant. I kept thinking about how frightened he must have been in the last moments of his young life. It was too awful to imagine, but it was true. One of our youth club members had been murdered in cold blood.

'You look like shite, Tone,' said Gerry as he left, still shaking.

I felt useless. One of our lads had just been murdered, the rest of the youth club members would be traumatised and just when I was needed most I could barely get out of bed. Lesley sensed my despair.

'Gerry came to see you at the very worst time,' she said.

'I hope I helped him,' I replied. 'I obviously couldn't help Billy.'

'His poor mother – she lost her husband too,' said Lesley.

'God love him,' I said. 'He was all talk, you know, but he was good-hearted underneath it all.'

'I know.'

'He just missed having a father and he got nothing but pain from this godforsaken country. And you've no idea how much those soldiers harassed that wee lad.'

'I know.'

We held each other and wept.

Dave Moser arrived looking shocked and distraught. Billy had been chatting with Dave in the Saltshaker just a few hours before his death – he had called into the café with his little niece who adored him. As the evening drew on, small groups of young people called round to our house. Many of us had been in this situation before. People in Belfast used to say, 'It doesn't really hit you how awful it all is until it comes to your own front door.' This pain had knocked on far too many front doors. Murder was part of the fabric of everyday life. Our fellow citizens were routinely slaughtered. All we could do on this horrific night was to be there for the stunned teenagers, to listen, to talk, to pray, to grieve with them and occasionally gently advise the angriest young people not to try to seek revenge, even though the desire was understandable.

'Do you think I should go to the wake?' I asked Lesley.

'Of course, if you're feeling well enough. Why wouldn't you go?'

I wasn't feeling well enough but that wasn't the issue.

'Do Billy's family really want a Protestant to come to the house, knowing what the last Protestants that came to that house did to Billy?'

'Do you want to go?'

'Yes, of course I do. I want to pay my respects and I want … and I want to see Billy.'

'Well, you go then. Go with some of the lads. Everyone knows you're the opposite of the people that did this.'

I asked Den and Jeff what I should do. They told me I should go because Billy loved the youth club. They advised me to buy a Mass Card, which was probably theologically dubious for a Presbyterian, but I didn't care. I went to the wake with some of the lads. I asked them to check with Billy's mother if she was okay with me being there. She told them she was glad I had come because her late son 'loved that oul Saltshaker'. This was peace in the midst of hatred, generosity in the face of evil. The house was dark and quiet, but full of people of all ages. Billy was lying in an open coffin in the same room where he had been murdered a few days before. He looked so young and innocent lying there. I always thought he looked older than his years but that day he looked younger. I had never seen anyone so young in a coffin before. It was so unfair. He deserved to be here and still alive. He deserved to meet a nice girl one day and get married and have children and die in his bed as an old man with his children and grandchildren around him. Billy never really got a chance. He was just one of so many young people who lost their lives to the hatred destroying this city. Billy was the first victim of 1988 and the 2,900th victim of the Troubles. He was only one of hundreds of young people, mostly forgotten victims of the Troubles, who never really got a chance at life. God forgive us!

I was deeply moved by the welcome I received from Billy's family and friends at the wake. There was kindness in the midst of great brutality. When I left the house I sat in the car with a small group of distraught youth club members. There was no teenage bravado or pretence here, just pure raw grief. I sat with my hands on the steering wheel staring out of the windscreen into the night and I wept with the lads.

A few days later I went to St Patrick's Chapel for my first funeral Mass. I had been in a Catholic church only a few times before. On the first such occasion I had secretly accepted the Mass at the Clonard Monastery Novena. It was the least Presbyterian moment of my life, and probably a sin from the perspective of both orthodox Catholics and Protestants. However this sad day was my first experience of an Irish Catholic funeral. I sat near the back of the church in an attempt to be unobtrusive in case any mourners objected to a Protestant at the requiem. It was a large funeral and I walked the streets of North Belfast behind Billy's coffin in the midst of a throng of mourners. As I followed the cortege with both Big Daves and a few other volunteers from the youth club I was aware that I must be one of only a tiny number of people from my side at the funeral. That day only confirmed my conviction that sides are irrelevant.

My conviction was further strengthened when the scenario I had feared since my first night at the Saltshaker Youth Club became a reality. It didn't happen exactly where and how I imagined it, but my nightmare of a drive-by shooting came true. Thankfully the youth club wasn't open that night but a group of the younger teenagers, many of them younger brothers of our senior youth club regulars, were standing outside the burger bar on the opposite side of the Antrim Road, when a vehicle drove past with a gunman shooting indiscriminately at the teenagers. Many were shot and injured. As soon as I heard the newsflash on the television I ran around the corner to see what had happened. The police and the army were on the scene and a fleet of ambulances was ferrying the injured teenagers to the hospital. This was Belfast in 1988, when teenagers hanging around outside a burger bar chatting about girls and football and Aha! were considered legitimate targets, in this case for the great cause of defending Ulster. For some reason the loyalist paramilitaries believed that a group of thirteen-year-olds eating chips and hamburgers were a threat to their Britishness, just like a sad nineteen-year-old lying sleeping on a sofa in his sitting room. Or maybe they just hated all Taigs.

When the bullets and the bombs ripped through the healthy bodies of our young people life became very basic. The focus wasn't on their life, their loves, their talent at sport or art, their education or their career. Their lives were reduced to the extent and location of their wounds. Panicking mothers and fathers frantically sought information about internal bleeding and surgery and blood transfusions. In these moments all that mattered was the bullet entry or the shrapnel wound. All life was reduced to minute-by-minute prospects of survival. Vulnerable young people with all of their potential, all of their loves and hopes and fears were reduced to flesh and blood and bones. That's what violence does to human beings. Motivated by great justifiable causes, violence dehumanises us, reducing us from unique, precious and talented souls to the bloody contents of an abattoir.

The stress and trauma of this disregard for human life was becoming unbearable for me and Lesley. Thousands of people in Belfast lived on the peace line for decades and just got on with their lives. They were obviously stronger than me. Maybe the future peace rested with the people who spent a lifetime here, who raised their children on the peace line, rather than people like me, parachuting in with my great ideals and burning out in a few short years, the zeal knocked out of me. I had to admit that with the exhaustion, the insecurity and the grief I wasn't sure if I could take much more. But I didn't want to give up either, just when the young people needed us most. Or maybe they didn't need me at all. Maybe we were just getting in the way. Maybe we were marginal influences, odd dissonant do-gooders whose influence was greater in our own minds and our fervent prayers than in any reality. I always thought I was strong. I had grown up in all of this. I had just survived my father's suicide. But I was beginning to feel that I didn't have the resilience and dedication to cope with all of this, to heal wounds that might never heal.

16

SHOCKS AND THREATS

I kissed Lesley farewell and patted Fara goodbye as I left for work that morning at 8.30 a.m. Lesley was in a good mood because she had applied for a new job as a fundraiser with the National Society for the Prevention of Cruelty to Children and had got an interview. Lesley still enjoyed her youth work and the young people in the Upper Shankill, but the funding was running out, and there are only so many games of Unihoc one person can referee without starting to feel slightly jaded. I was still waiting patiently to hear if my pilot programme on Downtown Radio would spawn a series – I lived in hope. As I made my way around the corner, through the security barrier, past the beleaguered Duncairn manse and church on to the Antrim Road and past the scorch-marked British army sanger, I was anticipating another normal day at the 174 Trust. Outside the Saltshaker Centre, the remains of another burnt-out vehicle were being removed from the main road and the new graffiti on the shutters of the drop-in centre was male genitalia rather than paramilitary propaganda.

John Evans led the prayer meeting with a reading from the Bible and a short thought for the day to inspire us for the hours of Christian service ahead. We shared information about the ups and downs of our work with each other – good news about a young man who was growing in his faith and bad news about an elderly woman who was dying of cancer. We prayed for each other and for the pensioners who were ill, the young people who were in prison and for the families of the victims of the latest bomb blast and shootings. If God had listened in advance to the Downtown Radio morning headlines he would have known exactly what suffering we were going to talk to him about.

After the morning prayer meeting I had a get-together with Dave Moser to discuss plans for some of our young people to spend a year with a Mennonite family in the USA. We believed it would be a life-changing opportunity for some of our young people who had difficult lives but great potential. I couldn't imagine anything so far away from the tensions of North Belfast as life with a family of peace-loving Christians in rural Indiana – and it seemed as if our plan was going to come to fruition. After the meeting I returned to preparing the latest issue of *Prayer News*, which we posted to our supporters across Northern Ireland and the world. I was interrupted several times by members of the unemployed club asking me to phone the dole office to help sort our their benefits. I was happy to help but it frustrated me that the staff in the social security office didn't sort out the problems so speedily when the teenagers themselves made the same telephone call. As I was finishing yet another pile of funding applications – this time for a summer camp in England, a new kitchen for the café and a new club for children with disabilities – I was suddenly disturbed by the boss.

'Tony, can I see you in my office now?' asked John.

This was unusual. John tended just to let me get on with my work. He knew I worked hard and always did my best and I think he trusted me. He managed the finances and the employment scheme, and I coordinated the youth work and the cross-community projects. If I were stuck I would take the initiative and knock on his door to ask for some wisdom or support. He often gave me advice on how to deal with various difficult scenarios that I was dealing with among the young people, whether it was drugs, abortion, homelessness, domestic violence or, in a surprise turn of events, Satanism up the Cavehill. But it was unusual for me to be called into his office.

'Darren's been arrested,' he said.

I didn't know Darren very well. He kept himself to himself. He was from a loyalist area of North Belfast and he was in his early twenties. Darren looked like a hard man but he didn't say much, and he had worked hard in the kitchen of the Saltshaker Café for several months. I assumed he had got into a fight at the weekend or been drunk and disorderly or joyriding or some other common youth crime.

'He's been arrested for a sectarian murder,' said John.

I was shocked and, for a moment, speechless.

'He's been charged with being involved in the killing of a Catholic last year,' said John.

I had never seen John look so troubled. 'UDA,' he added.

Fuck, I thought, but I didn't say it out loud.

I had recently thought that it couldn't get worse than your youth club members being shot in the street but I was wrong. One of the few Protestant staff working in a Christian centre in a mainly Catholic neighbourhood being charged with a sectarian murder of a Catholic was much, much worse. Yet again I felt sick to my stomach.

'I'm devastated,' said John putting his head in his hands. 'I employed him. I brought him here.'

'But how on earth were you to know that this would happen?' I said. 'How could anyone know this?'

John obviously had taken time to think through the possible repercussions of this news. Darren had been working in a cross-community staff team in our centre in a nationalist area where loyalist paramilitaries had been targeting Catholics, including one of our own youth club members. John explained that so far there was no suggestion that Darren had been involved in any incidents in the New Lodge since he had been working here which was only marginally reassuring. This was still a disaster for the 174 Trust.

'The IRA won't be too happy,' said John.

'Well I'm worried about that too, to tell you the truth,' I said.

A not-very-happy IRA usually led to bloodshed.

It dawned on me very quickly that there were ramifications for all of us at the Saltshaker Centre as a result of Darren's arrest. I had so many questions. Did he come here looking for potential victims among the people he worked with every day? Was he profiling the unemployed young people who frequented the café during the day for loyalist paramilitaries? Was he deliberately sent here? What would the lads think? What would the IRA think? Would the Provos suspect that we brought him here? Would they think we were running the centre as cover for a loyalist spy operation? What action would the IRA take? We were all at risk.

The 174 Trust's relationship with Sinn Féin had always been okay. We didn't ask for permission to be here but we were clearly permitted to be here. The local republican leadership must have discussed our presence and must have decided not to target us or burn us out or shoot any of the Protestants working in the centre. It seemed that the local powers in the New Lodge accepted we were genuine, harmless religious nutters who did some good work with the pensioners (including some of their mothers) and the young people (including some of their children). I would occasionally visit a local Sinn Féin councillor after a significant burglary to see if they could help us get our stuff back. He seemed surprised and slightly bemused that I wanted to talk to him but he was always helpful. But these circumstances were very different. We had allowed a loyalist paramilitary killer into their community for months. The men who decided who lived and who died in this community would be justifiably angry. Up until this point I was struggling with whether my work was making any real difference. It had never even crossed my mind that my mission might be doing more harm than good.

One by one, many of the local lads dropped into the centre. Darren's arrest had been on the Downtown Radio News.

'Have you heard about yer man, Darren?' each person asked in turn.

'The sleekit UDA bastard.'

'I know. It's awful,' was all I could say. 'It's terrible to think that he's been working here for all these months after what the police are saying he was involved in.'

'This is very bad for yousens.'

'Tone,' whispered Den, helpfully rather than threateningly. 'Make sure you're not here tonight. This whole fuckin' place is gonna be burned down.'

'Watch yerself, big lad,' advised Soup.

'If the RUC have been investigating Darren for a sectarian murder, why could they not just tell us as his employers and we could have removed him right away?' I asked John innocently. The concept of collusion did not even cross my mind.

I tried to defend the 174 Trust to the young people as best I could and explain how devastated John Evans and I were in the hope that some of them would speak up for us in the right circles and ask for mercy from the Provos. But I accepted that the Saltshaker Centre was going to be burned down. All of our work would be ashes by the next morning. Our stumbling attempts at peace building would be just another victim of violence begetting violence and destroying any seed of hope in a city addicted to retribution. My priority was to make sure that none of our staff or volunteers or young people would be in the building when the attack took place. I was also worried about our own house. Later in the day I was reassured without even having to ask.

'Your house is all right. You and Lesley are all right, Tone. It's this place that's gettin' it, so make sure no one is sleeping in them flats upstairs the night.'

Most of the young people seemed genuinely upset at the fate of the Saltshaker Centre because they knew very well that what had happened with Darren was the last thing that we would have wanted, and that they would ultimately lose having a place to go and having something to do if we got burnt out.

I slept even fewer hours than usual that night.

'Is anybody there?' Lesley asked with more urgency than usual as I checked the rear of the house several times through the night at the slightest sound. But the expected phone call to tell me that the centre had been petrol bombed never came. The next morning arrived and our centre was still there. For the next few days I was warned that the attack was coming that night but as each day passed it seemed that mercy had prevailed over anger. It was hard to understand exactly what had happened. It felt as if someone influential had intervened on our behalf. Maybe there was mercy in the IRA after all, or perhaps it might be considered bad PR to be killing well-meaning Christians again so soon after the Enniskillen bomb. The last thing the Provos needed was another Christian forgiving their barbarity in front of the world's media. Either that or all the threats had been a teenage testosterone exaggeration in the first place and the republican leadership of North Belfast had more important acts to execute.

However some of the young people would never trust us again. I had stuck a photograph of a camping trip with Billy and the lads on the wall of my office. For weeks after Darren's arrest I had to explain that this photograph was taken by me and had never left my office. The word on the street was that the photograph was being used by loyalist paramilitaries to target the young people one by one for a horrific death, in the style of a plot line from a horror film. Thankfully no one else came to harm, but the whole incident proved to some of the young people that, even though we were well-meaning Christians, we were still Prods and ultimately we simply couldn't be trusted. The Belfast mindset had returned to its default – there are some good ones, but you can't really trust them. I was feeling more and more that, in spite of my natural optimism and inextinguishable sense of hope, it would be impossible to make any lasting changes around here.

17

TIME TO GO

The first few months of 1988 had been traumatic. For years, Lesley and I had agreed that we didn't want to be a nice middle-class couple with a bungalow and a hatchback car and a lawnmower – but now the prospect was very attractive indeed. My vision of other peace-loving Christians joining us to live on the peace line was a distant dream. Volunteers came and went at the 174 Trust but no one else bought a house in the area. Other staff didn't even have to live within a mile of the centre any more. We decided that I should begin to look for a new job, doing similar work, but a position that would allow me to come home from work in the evening and forget about it for a few hours.

Lesley did a brilliant interview and got the job as a regional fundraiser for the NSPCC, which meant she earned nearly twice as much as me and got a company car. Her region was the west of Northern Ireland, which she knew very well, but living in Belfast was an inconvenience and she had many long car journeys in her company Vauxhall Astra taking boxes for flag days to Enniskillen and Derry.

By the spring of 1988 my mother had got to a stage in her

grieving process when she was prepared to let go of some of my father's belongings. The family garage was full of hundreds of tools my father had amassed during a lifetime of working as a foreman in the foundry and my mother asked me if I wanted any of them. With my limited DIY skills and interest I had little use for them but, as I searched through the dusty boxes of tools, I had an idea. If I gave some of the tools to some of the lads in the unemployed club it would give them a start in developing a small business. After all the terrible times with losing Billy and Darren's arrest I thought this would be a good way of building some hope for the future. I shared the idea in the unemployed club and both Gerry and Paddy expressed enthusiasm. We agreed that I would donate my father's tools to help them to get started. I firmly believed in the wise proverb often quoted in relation to community development that if you give a man a fish he is hungry again in an hour but if you teach him to catch a fish you do him a good turn. I was giving Paddy and Gerry a fishing rod. The lads accompanied me to gather the tools together and they popped in to the house to say hello to my mother.

'I'm very sorry about your husband,' said Gerry respectfully.

My mother offered to make the lads a nice cuppa tea, and a Marie biscuit, which they politely declined. Afterwards they expressed surprise at the lack of flags and loyalist symbols in my mother's house, although they thought her Charles and Diana wedding plate was lovely, so it was. They noticed my mother's royal souvenir on the wall of her living room as something different in the same way I noticed the Sacred Heart of Jesus on the wall of their houses. We focused on gathering up the best tools in the garage.

A few weeks later I met up with the lads to check how the new business was going and to see if they had secured a good customer base in the local community. It became clear that the start-up had not started. I was reliably informed that Gerry and Paddy had sold the tools for drink. It was the final straw for me. I was giving far too much of my time, my resources and my life for very little in return. At best I was making very little difference, at worst I was doing more harm than good. In this instance I suspected I was being manipulated and used by young people who ultimately thought I deserved everything I got for the audacity of parachuting into their community in the first place.

There was good news when I finally heard from Downtown Radio that I was going to be trained as a presenter with a view to launching my first series of *Rockspel* in the autumn. My pilot had been well received and it seemed that I might have a broadcasting career after all. Lesley and I were so delighted that we celebrated with our favourite KFC variety meal in a Glengormley car park. I couldn't wait to announce to the youth club that I was going to be a radio presenter and to make the point that you could be anything you wanted to be if you really put your mind to it.

'Class!' said Jeff.

'Well done, Tone,' said Gerry.

'Here, are you gonna be famous nigh, Tony?' asked Patsy. 'I can tell everyone I knew you when you were nathin', so I can.'

Not all of the reactions fed my ego.

'DJs are wankers,' commented Michael.

'Aye, hang the DJ!' added Tonto.

The young people sang the chorus of Morrissey's 'Hang the DJ' every few minutes for the rest of the night.

A few months later I applied for a job with the National Council of YMCAs, to support YMCAs throughout Ireland who were working with socially disadvantaged young people in local communities up and down the country and on both sides of the border. The job would allow me to share my hard-earned experience in other places, across communities and across borders, and I could try to make a difference on a bigger scale. I could also go home at night and be a better husband and try to forget about work. After a demanding interview with men in blazers, to my great surprise I got the job. Lesley was delighted and to celebrate we went upmarket for a monumental meal at the popular new carvery in the Barclay restaurant at Shaw's Bridge. Our lives were beginning to change but I felt guilty about the prospect of leaving the 174 Trust. On the one hand I was moving on to a great new opportunity but on the other hand I feared I was giving up on North Belfast too soon. When I handed in my resignation both Rev. Taylor and John Evans said they were disappointed and sad to see me go. However their immediate plans to recruit my successor from the pool of committed volunteers, proved to me the meaning of the phrase I had often heard that 'no one is indispensable'. Dave Moser was similarly sad but not surprised as I had shared my thoughts about the future with him. I would miss my first fellow pacifist co-worker and now that I was leaving the 174 Trust we pledged we would stay in touch no matter where we went in the future. This was no idle 'let's keep in touch' – the friendship and spirituality of Big Dave, my Mennonite friend from Indiana, would remain with me forever.

I wasn't looking forward to telling the lads in the youth club that I was leaving. On the first Tuesday night youth club after I had handed in my resignation I gathered all the young people around the pool table.

'I've something to tell you, lads,' I said seriously. 'I'm leavin' here to start a new job.'

Michael put down his pool cue. 'Ach, Tone!' he said, and then took his next shot.

I was hoping at least one person would be devastated.

'Are you sleggin'?' asked Soup.

'No, I'm not sleggin', I've got a new job in the YMCA.'

'Always thought you were a faggot as well as a speccy bastard!' he replied.

There followed an impromptu performance of the Village People's 'YMCA' on top of the pool table complete with the actions, which of course damaged the top of the pool table and descended into scuffles.

'Scuffles!' shouted Tonto.

Sometimes it felt as though nothing had changed since my very first night in charge. Once calm was restored I continued with my important announcement.

'I'll still be living round the corner for a while and I'll be a volunteer on a Tuesday night, so I'm not disappearing,' I explained, trying to soften the impact of my news as much as possible.

The youth club continued that night as if nothing much had happened. A few of the young people came up to me and shook my hand and said thank you. I was genuinely touched by these sincere gestures. Over the years I had taught a few of the young people to play the guitar. I had taught them the basic chords and then they had gone on to practise hard and learn by themselves and they turned out to be much better and more talented guitar players than me. My prayer was that a few of the ideas I had shared about faith and love and hope might bear similar fruit in their lives.

Later that night, as I was checking all the doors and locking up the centre, Den approached me.

'Why are you leavin', Tone?' he asked

'Well, Den, this is not the sort of job you can do forever.' I explained.

'I'd love a job like yours,' he said. 'Sure you just sit around and play pool all day.'

'Come on, Den, you know there's a lot more to it than that.'

'Only sleggin',' he replied.

I gave him a friendly pat on the back.

'Well, any job at all would do me,' he said sadly.

'You'll be all right, Den,' I said. 'I'm sure you'll get a job one day – you're a good lad, so you are. Most of youse round here are good lads.'

'Everyone leaves us you know,' said Den.

I could see tears in his eyes. He appeared to be filling up.

'What do you mean?' I asked.

'All youse youth workers come and tell us how important we all are to you, and say you'd do anything to help us out but youse all leave us in the end. You're just the same as all the others and the next one will be just the same as you.'

I had no reply to this. Den was probably right. I put my arm around his shoulder and walked him out of the front door of the Saltshaker Centre and on to the paint-splattered footpath on the Antrim Road. It seemed like only yesterday that that police-propelled paint bomb had landed at our feet and he had commenced my education about living on the other side.

'Well, I hope I made a bit of difference,' I said.

Den looked over at the British army watchtower where a pair of eyes and a gun were pointing in our direction.

'Don't worry, Tone – there's hundreds of years of British oppression to deal with round here. It's gonna take a long time, so it is.'

Lesley and I made the decision that the time was right to put our little house up for sale. In the first few days there was no interest, in the next few weeks there was no interest, and in the following few months there was still no interest. Not a single viewing. Lesley's prediction was right. No one wanted to buy a little house on the peace line, especially as the houses at the end of the row still had boarded-up windows from the latest sectarian attacks. By the summer of 1988 I had started my new job, and Lesley was driving miles around the country for the NSPCC, but we still couldn't sell the house. We asked our solicitor and the Co-Ownership Association if it was possible to get a bridging loan so that we could move but the rules made it impossible. I asked Rev. Taylor and John Evans if the 174 Trust would consider buying our house to use as a home for volunteers, but they decided to buy a much bigger house on the Cliftonville Road instead. Our vision of a community of radical Christians living on the peace line to witness and work for peace was gone. We were left with faded dreams and an unsaleable house. All our idealism had come to this. Every day we prayed for a solution to our problem and then, when we had almost given up hope, we received a phone call from the estate agent. The good news was that a couple wanted to view the house that evening. We frantically tidied every room from top to bottom, which took about an hour, and put some pot pourri in our best Ainsley dish to make the house at least smell desirable. Fara was banished to the garden. When the couple arrived they explained that they had relatives living just across the road. So when I said, 'It's lovely. It's very quiet round here too, so it is', the prospective buyers gave me a 'who do you think you are kidding' look. However within only a few hours they put in an offer and we accepted so swiftly that our desperation must have been obvious. We were finally relieved that we would not be living there for the rest of our lives.

A few months later I returned to the house for the last time. We were now living with Lesley's parents in Bellaghy for a few months until we could move into our bungalow in Magherafelt. It was my turn to move into Lesley's territory.

All our furniture was in storage. There were no curtains on the windows and, as the electricity had already been switched off, the rooms were lit up only by the blurry orange glow of the security lights from the army barracks. I walked through every room and reflected on the past three years in the home in which our married life began. I remembered the day in my bedroom that I heard that Billy had died; the day of my father's inquest at Crumlin Road Courthouse when my family had gathered here; the evening we brought Fara home for the first time; the day our neighbour had kidnapped 'the fuckin' mutt'; and the day she gave birth to a litter of pups. I remembered the lunchtimes with Lesley watching *Neighbours* and the evenings I enjoyed in front of the television earnestly attempting to introduce Dave Moser to the wonders of *Doctor Who*. And when I went upstairs I thought again of all the sleepless nights when Lesley had asked, 'Is there anybody there?'

Finally, after revisiting every room, I sat on the green carpet in the living room where so many different feet had trod over the past three years. I was thankful for all that we had achieved and even hopeful that some of our work might have made a difference. I was no longer the naive idealistic young man who had moved into this area three years ago, but I was still an optimist and I retained a deep-seated hope that all our work had not been in vain. I prayed to God and thanked him for keeping us safe and asked him to bless and protect all the youth workers that would come after me to continue the work of the 174 Trust as well as the young people from the New Lodge who were at the heart of everything I'd done or tried to do. After a long time sitting in the orange glow I got up and walked towards the front door with tears in my eyes. Strangely I think they were tears of joy. I was happy to have started out with Lesley in this house. I was glad to have survived the past three years and I was excited about the future. I closed the door behind me for the very last time and said goodbye to the little house on the peace line.

EPILOGUE

BACK TO THE FUTURE

It's thirty years since I was married, thirty years since my father died and thirty years since we lived on what is now referred to as a North Belfast interface. A great deal has changed in my life since the day last year that I climbed up Divis Mountain and decided to write this book. Both of my beautiful daughters have moved away to live in England and my mother passed away exactly two months ago – I returned to the summit of the Black Mountain a few weeks ago for the scattering of her ashes. My mother was eighty-three years old when she died and had suffered from cancer for the last ten years. Every day for the past two months I have replayed the final hours of her life in my mind. We held her hand, mopped her brow, played songs to her, comforted her and prayed with her. We told her not to worry about us, we said it was okay for her to let go and most of all we told her how much we loved her. On the night she died I felt I needed to take something of hers with me before I kissed her goodbye. I lifted the Bible that always sat on her bedside table and took it home with me. At the back of the little black book I found a small plastic wallet with an assortment of fragile yellowed newspaper clippings, which had been carefully cut out from the death notices of the *Belfast Telegraph* over a period of forty years, death notices for my granny and granda and all those dear family and friends that had passed on before my mother. But then I came upon a very different piece of paper, a small scrap of blue paper with torn irregular edges, folded over once. I knew immediately what I had discovered. It was my father's suicide note, scribbled in pen and with familiar smudges from the tears that stained the ink, exactly as I remembered it from the first and last time I had read it on 20 May 1986. I was shocked. Twenty-five years ago my mother told me that she had destroyed the suicide note because a counsellor had advised her that holding on to it would prevent her recovery. I had believed her.

As I drive along the motorway lost in my memories, I take the wrong exit. My navigating skills haven't improved much. I am endlessly grateful for Google Maps. I'm aware that I am still grieving the loss of my mother but this bereavement feels different. I've only ever lost a parent to suicide before. This is a different type of grief. I don't feel guilty. I'm not angry with my mother. I'm not feeling guilty for feeling angry. I'm not trying to recall the warning signs I missed. I'm not blaming myself for not doing enough and for not being there that morning. I'm not tortured by the thought of the desperation and unhappiness that led to the death. I'm not confused and shocked and shaken to the core. I think back to my experiences of thirty years ago. Unlike my mother's recent passing, my father was in the depths of despair and alone in the final hours of his life. There was no one there to hold his hand or mop his brow, to comfort him or pray with him. There was no one there to tell him how much we needed him, to beg him not to let go and to tell him just how much we loved him. I still think of my father every day and the fact that he took his own life is a part of me. I don't want one more woman to experience what my mother went through. I don't want one more son to experience what I went through. Today I volunteer as the chair of the board of trustees of Contact, a counselling charity that provides a twenty-four-hour telephone lifeline for people in crisis and despair in Northern Ireland. I believe that every suicide is preventable up until the last moment of life and today I do what I can to contribute to the goal of 'zero suicide' in a city with an unacceptably high rate that is partly a legacy of the Troubles. Later this month I'm going to give the opening address at a major suicide prevention conference in the new Titanic Conference Centre in Belfast. I'm holding on to my idealism. I'm still trying to make a difference where I can, hoping my contribution will help to reduce loss and suffering. However, over the years I've become more of a pragmatic optimist than a zealous idealist. I'm not as naive as I was in 1986 but I have worked hard over many years in peace building and social action to avoid becoming cynical.

We were in such a state of shock at my father's funeral that we just wanted to survive the day but my mother's funeral was a good time to say goodbye to both of my dear parents. My father's memorial tree grows taller every year in the gardens at Roselawn Cemetery and in the next few weeks the rest of my mother's ashes will be interred there to be with him forever. I often reflect on all that my father missed out on over this last thirty years. He never got to see me married. He missed out on the joys of meeting all his beautiful grandchildren. He didn't get to enjoy the fruits of his labours in the foundry, such as his son becoming a successful author. He had no idea that people of different ages and faiths from different countries would one day say, 'I really liked your father', 'Your father was a strong independent-minded man' and 'Your dad must have inspired you'. My father would never hear me reply thirty years after he left us, 'It's taken me all this time to work out that he inspired me more than I ever imagined'.

As I drive through familiar Belfast streets towards Clifton Park Avenue my mind returns once again to that night in 1977 when my parents won the ballroom dancing competition in Butlin's in Mosney. I play their song 'The Last Waltz'. As I turn into Brucevale and arrive back at the little house I have an image in my mind of my parents reunited, holding hands and dancing again, a last waltz that will go on forever.

I have automatically parked exactly where I used to leave the rusting Renault 5. I notice that all of the graffiti on the wall opposite the row of houses has been painted over with purple paint. No more INLA or IRA or KAP. In fact there are no obvious signs to claim that this street belongs to one side or the other. It immediately feels normal, lighter and less oppressive than I remember. A young woman passes me pushing a high-tech buggy and two children are happily playing a game in one of the tiny gardens. The sun is shining through the clouds and a gentle breeze blows autumn leaves along the road. Some of the houses still have the original windows and doors but most, including our former little house, have new white PVC frames and doors. The houses at the end of the row have no broken windows and have a pleasant outlook onto green space. But twenty years after the

IRA ceasefire, this is still the peace line. The reality is that this tiny park serves as a visually pleasing barrier to the other side. On the other side of the railings is a fence, and then another fence and then another one. So many fences! As I turn on to Clifton Park Avenue I can still see the footprint of the long demolished cats' home at the rear of our old house. All that remains is grass and a few of the trees where thousands of cats once climbed, but the site is completely surrounded by a high metal fence. I remember the Robert Frost poem 'Mending Wall' that I studied in my English class at Belfast Royal Academy just around the corner: 'Good fences make good neighbors'.

It was an ironic line in the poem, but Belfast has taken it literally. The reality is that good fences make mistrusting neighbours feel safer. But it seems very peaceful here this morning and I feel no fear. It appears that the people of North Belfast have settled for peaceful co-existence with reassuring fences, rather than choosing to integrate and flourish together without barriers. Frost wrote:

> Before I built a wall I'd ask to know
> What I was walling in or walling out,
> And to whom I was like to give offence.
> Something there is that doesn't love a wall.

There is something within me that hates a wall. Years after the Good Friday Agreement it is clear that replacing solid peace walls with fencing is regarded as progress in Belfast. If you can see the other side you're more likely to consider them human beings just like you. I supposed that's a good start.

As result of living here I went on to work in peace building across many other interfaces for many years and in 2008 I wrote a discussion paper proposing 'A Five Phase Process for Removing Peace Walls in Northern Ireland'. A few people, keen to keep the segregated status quo, responded predictably. A North Belfast MLA proclaimed 'Them walls will never come down'. Several judgmental North Belfast community workers who were busy polishing their weapons in 1987 when I was living here and bringing young people together on this peace line asked, 'What would yer man know about living on the peace line anyway?' And a member of staff of the government-funded Community Relations Council for Northern Ireland asked who the fuck I thought I was. However, in spite of the naysayers protecting their various fiefdoms, my proposal was well received by most people including many of the elected representatives who acknowledged that these walls are also barriers to jobs and prosperity in the poorest neighbourhoods of Belfast that suffered the most during the conflict. Today, due mainly to a huge amount of work by youth and community organisations over many years, it is now the Stormont government's policy to remove all of the peace walls by 2023. That's a dismantling I will enjoy. But it will only happen when the people living beside them feel safe enough. I understand this completely from my own personal experience. The removal of the wall in Clifton Park Avenue, albeit to be replaced with a million fences, is a big step in the right direction. As I look around me I notice that the fences are separated by a patchwork of well-kept lawns. That really sums us up in Belfast – stubborn steel fences and beautiful green grass. The best of us and the worst of us, side by side on the peace line; green grass representing the softness and beauty of this land and black metal fences representing our steely ingrained divisions.

In spite of the fences, the things that strike me most are the wide-open spaces and the newly built Girdwood Community Hub. The army barracks with its massive perimeter security wall and searing spotlights is gone. In fact today you can see the whole way to the rear of Crumlin Road Gaol, now a top tourist attraction. The £20 million Girdwood Community Hub has been hailed by Belfast City Council as 'a state-of-the-art shared space hub which offers first-class leisure, community and education facilities'. Inside is a multitude of 'shared spaces' for local people from either side of the fences to come and interact with each other, if they really want to. It's an ambitious project and I hope it works. The politicians are still fighting over whether the remaining vacant land around it should be used to build Catholic houses or Protestant houses because there are still plenty of votes in fighting for denominational housing for your own side. Today the community hub looks pretty empty. Once the not very state-of-the-art fences all around the state-of-the-art shared space start disappearing we will know that all this money has been well spent. My vision is of shared streets around this hub with no fences at all and I don't care whether the houses are Protestant or Catholic or even state of the art – as long as good people are once again living together as neighbours in an integrated community without fear of the other side. With this expensive symbol of hope in front of me I walk back and forward across the peace line several times. I feel no sense of danger here at all today. It's an imperfect peace but I feel a strong sense of hope for the future from the obvious progress in my former neighbourhood.

I walk towards the front door of our former house and peek through the familiar black diagonal wooden fence that I once painted every year. There is a satellite dish and gas piping on the outside wall, bringing natural gas and satellite TV into the house where once only coal and four analogue channels were received. The tiny garden is only half the size it was in 1986 because now the house has a pretty conservatory and stylish decking attached to it. When I lived here I was more concerned about getting a very different kind of decking in that back garden. The house is bigger, more attractive and safer today. However, now I notice how close together the houses are. In the 1980s this gave a sense of closeness and security but today I feel a little claustrophobic.

I decide to walk around the corner, to retrace my daily walk to work at the Saltshaker Centre on the Antrim Road. The area on my right-hand side is a bright and open space without the huge brooding barracks. I can see the whole way up to Divis Mountain. There is no sign of the Troubles except the faded pink 'Control Zone Ends' sign on one of the lampposts. During the conflict this sign indicated that you were leaving a control zone and that you could now park your car. Most of the streets around Girdwood army barracks had been control zones to prevent car and mortar bombs. This forgotten and outdated sign reminds me of the strange 'Give Way' sign I spotted on my trek to the top of Divis Mountain last year. This is no longer a control zone. The military may well be gone, but so many of the housing estates in this city are still under the control of gangs of men who have controlled them for decades, and who still brutalise anyone who dares to disobey them. I'd love to see the end of these control zones too. I'd like to see every neighbourhood given back to the ordinary people who have suffered enough. Many local residents feel the same way about the paramilitaries, even if they are related to them, but feel powerless to speak out. They really have to watch themselves round here you know.

I arrive at the former Duncairn Presbyterian Manse and Church. It's an incredible sight – the 174 Trust is still going strong and the old church, long closed as a place of Presbyterian worship, has been transformed beautifully into the Duncairn Centre for Culture & Arts for all the people of the city. I've been back here before at cross-community youth initiatives, music concerts and peace conferences. I've even given a few book readings here at 'Scribes at the Duncairn', which is part of a fantastic community-based reading initiative, of which I'm proud to be a patron. The centre has become a genuinely shared space where everyone has a voice, and feels respected and welcomed. Lesley, Dave Moser and I have returned here for a few reunions where we met some of our former youth club members. It was good to reconnect and to hear how they have created good lives for their families. I enjoyed hearing about their jobs, the achievements of their children and stories of how the youth workers at the Saltshaker influenced their lives at a time when so much was stacked against them. Maybe our short years on the peace line made a little difference after all.

Living here had a huge impact on me. It has led me to the belief that neither a utopian United Ireland nor a beloved British Ulster was worth a single drop of blood. I'm disturbed when I hear histories of the Troubles which justify the violence and airbrush the sheer bloody brutality. I've concluded that every precious human life destroyed was worth a billion times more than either nation.

On this day I'm feeling ever more hopeful when I turn the corner on to the main Antrim Road. The British army watchtower has been replaced with a sunbed-tanning studio with luxury apartments above. When I arrive at 174 Antrim Road I find it is now a taxi depot and attractive-looking flats. A lot has changed in thirty years and most of it for the better.

As I return to my car it starts to rain. I feel teary-eyed thinking about the loss of my parents, the loss of so many young people like Billy, the loss of my own idealistic youth. I'm feeling deep love for the young woman who moved here with me in 1986 and who is still my wife. But I realise that most of these are tears of joy. I'm feeling more hopeful than I expected. The continued divisions in this city frustrate me hugely but today, here and now, all around me I see more signs of a hopeful future than of a brutal past. I dry my tears and drive off in the direction of the Crumlin Road. As I pass the gaol I wonder whether any of the construction workers involved in transforming the prison into a tourist attraction found a pair of red plastic 1980s ladies spectacles hidden under the floorboards in Seamie's former cell. On my right is the Crumlin Road courthouse where my father's inquest was held. It is the exact opposite of the gaol – burnt out, ugly, derelict and neglected. This section of the Crumlin Road is a good representation of Northern Ireland today – in part transformed, but with some aspects stubbornly unchanged.

The naive idealism of thirty years ago was knocked out of me back then, but not my faith or hopes for a better future and for a city without walls. Today I still believe in the possibility of a land where our children and grandchildren will live together in the same streets and play together on the same teams. I dream that one day the children of this city will learn together in history classes in the same schools about something called a 'peace line' and structures called 'peace walls' that once divided their beautiful thriving city but are now a sad and distant memory. And that no one has to watch themselves round here any more.

ACKNOWLEDGEMENTS

I want to acknowledge all the support I have received from bookstores, libraries, festivals, voluntary groups, universities and schools, both at home and abroad.

Special thanks to George Heslin of the 1st Irish Festival and the W.B. Yeats Society of New York City for hosting the first public reading from this book, and to the Arts Council of Northern Ireland for supporting my travel costs. I also want to thank Dr Brian Logue for arranging my book reading at the Keough-Naughton Institute for Irish Studies at the University of Notre Dame, Jean and Tanner Kling for organising my first book tour in Los Angeles, and Maricolette Walsh for inviting me to Literary Corner at Milwaukee Irish Fest. Finally I want to thank my dear friends David and Ingrid Moser in Goshen, Indiana, for their constant encouragement, support and hospitality during my book tours to the USA.

I want to acknowledge the continued encouragement, support and advice of my literary agents, Paul and Susan Feldstein.

Last but not least, thanks to Patsy Horton, Helen Wright (my brilliant editor) and Michelle Griffin at Blackstaff Press for their enthusiasm and advice, hard work and warm support in publishing *Little House on the Peace Line*.